ABOUT THE AUTHOR

I've always been around bikes. As a child I spent many hours on the back of my father's Honda CB400N Superdream, BMW R80/7, then BMW R100RT, travelling from Manchester across the Pennines and the occasional day trip to Wales.

In 1984, at the age of sixteen and serving an electrical apprenticeship, I bought a Honda MT5. Since the previous owner had tinkered with the exhaust baffles, I could get the best part of 40mph out of it but soon moved on to a new Honda MBX125F. Two years later, though, I had bought a car and sold the bike.

In 1991, with some time on my hands and regretting not having passed my full bike licence, I took the test and passed, although it would be many years later that I would buy a bike. Some twenty-two years later, now working as an IT consultant and with my two children grown up, I bought a Kawasaki ZX636 A1P and a year later traded it in against a BMW S1000RR.

As the distances increased from the weekend day trips to weeks away in the Scottish Highlands, it was time to change, and the sport bike rider became an adventure bike rider. In 2016, the RR was traded for a R1200GS Triple Black, on which I have travelled on many a weekend adventure in the British Isles, and occasionally, much further afield.

Are We Doing the Stelvio Today?

Seven Riders Tour the Alps

Enjoy the Ride

Matu

Martin Smith

The Book Guild Ltd

First published in Great Britain in 2020 by

The Book Guild Ltd
9 Priory Business Park
Wistow Road, Kibworth
Leicestershire, LE8 0RX
Freephone: 0800 999 2982
www.bookguild.co.uk
Email: info@bookguild.co.uk
Twitter: @bookguild

Typeset in 12pt Jensen Pro

Printed and bound by CPI Group (UK) Ltd, Croydon, CR0 4YY

ISBN 978 1913208 547

British Library Cataloguing in Publication Data.
A catalogue record for this book is available from the British Library.

To my wife Jayne
for tolerating my disappearances

Contents

Preface

I'm an adventure bike rider. I bought the bike; I bought the suit; I bought the boots. I am an adventurer. Right?

Despite this, much of my 'adventure' takes place at the weekend through the hills and valleys of the British countryside. I travel from tearoom to tearoom, and I'm not alone. On any given Saturday or Sunday, in any given rural location, you will find motorcycles travelling on the country lanes that would be just as comfortable crossing the wilds of Africa or the jungles of Asia.

We all read the magazine articles and we read the occasional overland travel book, but for many of us the closest we get to broaden our horizons is an annual motorcycle trip across Europe. Our jobs, families and other commitments mean we must keep the round-the-world trip in a shelved box labelled 'pipe dream' next to our copies of Ewan McGregor and Charlie Boorman DVDs.

In the pages that follow, part-story and part-guidebook, this is the tale of one of these journeys. We are the guys that sit between the day-trippers and the overland adventurers. We show that you can find inspiration and exploration without leaving civilisation behind or forsaking a comfy hotel bed for a camp bed. I hope that I can show you that you can still adventure on a budget and keep the day job.

The chosen destination is one of the most popular for two-wheeled travellers and takes us across the Swiss, French and Italian Alps.

Introducing the Travellers (In Their Own Words)

Nick Smallwood

My first bike was a Honda SS50 (1976), and it could not have been a worse bike to introduce me to biking. It was slow, heavy and very basic. I bought it off my brother's friend for £123. Having said all that, I wish I still had it today, as they are being sold for upward of £3,000.

My next bike was a Yamaha RD 200 (stroker). I loved that bike, as it was the start of the big leagues, fast for the time, and that lovely two-stroke smell. I was never home, out on the bike all the time with friends, riding anything from a CB250 to a KH250. At that time, you could ride anything on L-plates up to a 250cc.

By the time the '70s had finished, I was in a full-time job, with all the responsibilities that went along with that. So, the biking had to be put on hold until 2013, when Brian and I finally made the decision that we would take our tests, and so the love of biking started all over again.

I passed the test and bought Honda 600 Hornet, which I had for two weeks, but while in a BMW Motorrad dealer, I saw a lovely white RT 1200 which I just had to have. When BMW decided to launch the S1000XR I knew that was the new bike for me. I had two XRs (having been knocked off the first one) over a four-year period.

Brian Jones

As a sixteen-year-old electrical apprentice, I bought my first motorcycle. A purple Yamaha FS1E moped (affectionately known as a Fizzy 50). As soon as I was seventeen, I upgraded to the biggest machine available without passing a test: the mighty Suzuki GT 250 Ram Air. Almost good for 100 miles an hour. Then came girlfriends and cars, and I lost touch with my inner biker.

Thirty-six years later, Nick and I were at race meeting, being boring old farts, lamenting the fact that we would really like to get back into biking. We hadn't, however, passed our test, so without a licence, forget it.

When Nick's son Ben told us to stop moaning and that a fast-pass scheme would take less than a week for us to get through, both Nick and I had no answer to this, so we did it.

It took me a couple of attempts to get through the first module of the practical test, but then I was let loose on a Suzuki 650, my first big bike.

Eighteen months later, I upgraded to a proper big bike, a BMW K1300S. I ride mostly day trips, with the occasional weekend away or full-blown European tour.

Dan Russell

As a child growing up in Indiana, my favourite matchbox car was a dirt bike. For as long as I can remember, I've been fascinated by motorcycles in particular but would go out of my way to ride anything with handlebars. Motorcycles, dirt bikes, three- and four-wheel ATVs, and jet skis. If it had handlebars, I'd ride the tits off it.

At thirteen, I convinced my dad to teach me to ride his 1976 Honda 350 street bike. The deal was I had to be able to get it to run first. I don't believe he thought I'd actually ever be able to get it to start. Once I was finally able to kick that old thing to life, though, I was off to the races. Flying around the farm and across the fields with a sense of freedom I'd never known before and have been chasing ever since.

I rode that bike for about a year before my teenage exuberance caught up with me while my cousin was on the back, resulting in a spectacular crash with the bike flying through the air and being totalled. Luckily the worst injuries either of us had was a broken nose, chipped tooth, grazed face and forearms, and a slightly bruised ego. Luckily all suffered by me, as my back cushioned her landing during the crash.

After that I was bike-less for a couple years, until at sixteen, against my parents' wishes, I bought my own dirt bike. A Suzuki DR250. I spent many days racing up and down the back roads and exploring the forests around where I grew up. I had countless exciting adventures on that old bike. That lasted until I was newly married, and we needed the money, so the bike had to go.

It wasn't until several years later that I met Shane and rode his SV650. The desire for another bike had always been there, but other things in life had been taking precedence until then. Riding Shane's bike instantly rekindled the need for another motorcycle. A 2009 ZX6R was purchased. That lead to an obsession with sport bikes, canyon carving and track days… many amazing friends have been made because of the purchase of that first ninja. It led to my wife learning to ride and getting her own bike. And to a Suzuki V-Strom 650 for adventures around the US.

Shane McKerchie

I grew up a farm kid in Michigan doing everything outdoors: hunting, fishing, dirt bikes, snowmobiles and water sports.

My first street bike was a Suzuki SV 650 and subsequently

a Honda CBR 900, Kawasaki ZX6R, and I've had or ridden several others.

Now aged thirty-three and married with three daughters, I am a paramedic firefighter based in Indiana. Being a paramedic has certainly come in useful. I suppose you could call me the fall guy of the group and have used my experience to patch myself up a number of times.

This was my first trip to Europe and my first motorcycle tour as well. Past events have been trail rides on dirt and some motocross tracks, US129 dragon trips and track days. This trip was one of the best adventures of my lifetime and I can't wait until the next one.

Greg Atherton

I'm a military man of South Carolina and I maintain Apache helicopters to fund my hobbies.

I grew up outdoors and as is tradition for young men with access to some land and too much free time, dirt bikes became my first motorised two-wheeled habit.

As age and access to bigger toys increased, I bought a 2003 ZX6R, which was my first road-going motorcycle. It was taken right across the eastern side of the US for 60,000 miles before being sold for an upgrade to a 2015 S1000RR.

The tour of the Alps is my first civilian trip through Europe, and certainly won't be the last.

Eddie Printz

While travelling in the rear-facing seat of my family's huge wood-grained 1977 Ford LDT-2 station wagon as a child, I would be grinning ear to ear when a motorcycle was within sight. If you're a biker, you know which kids will grow up to ride just by the shit-eating grin they have when they see a motorcyclist. They can't help it, it's inside them and most don't know it, but life will propel them towards their first motorcycle.

My first motorcycle was a small matchbox Honda Enduro at age seven, which I still own. I started working a paper route at age nine on my bicycle and quickly added more customers than I could handle in one trip. I saved my money and dreamt of the day I was old enough to own a moped. I cut my teeth on a minibike with no suspension in a dirt field.

Then I moved up to the Honda 'Big Red': three wheels of death. Then came horses just before I turned fifteen, and I was able to look for my first two-wheeled ticket to freedom. My neighbour had just gotten his first car and agreed to sell me his French Motobécane moped. It had a belt drive and an upswept silver muffler on a metallic blue frame with a two-stroke engine. Freedom was mine and the fire was lit! I would use that moped to build that paper route to a morning and afternoon business, and by the time I was seventeen I had saved enough money to buy a real motorcycle.

The Honda dealer knew who I was when I walked into the showroom. They know that shit-eating grin too. I was hypnotised by the new red, white and blue Honda interceptors, but when the dealer figured out how much money I had saved, he took me to the back corner of the showroom where a few of the leftovers were parked. There sat matching black and red 1984 Honda V-twin 500 Ascots under a thin coat of dust. I picked the black one, and my sister, who was eighteen at the time, had to sign before they would take my fat stack of small, wrinkled bills.

I rode, crashed, wrenched and repeated until the late '90s. The old Ascot had a lot of miles, as I would ride it everywhere and for a time it was my only transportation, even in the snow. For a short time, I rode a huge Thoroughbred Motorsports Trike with a truck engine in it, before selling it for a 1995 Ducati Monster 900. Then came a string of bikes: a yellow SV650; a black Aprilia Mana; a silver BMW GT750; a fully restored 1986 candy apple Honda V-65 Magna; a 1986 red, white and blue V-4 1000 interceptor; and a pair of red, white and blue 750 interceptors for a future restoration. Then came my first track bike, a 2006 Kawasaki 636. I currently ride a 2008 Ducati Multistrada 1100s, and 2012 Pikes Peak 1100s Multistrada.

I'm a veteran and an attorney based in the Blue Ridge Mountains of North Carolina, and I have been riding motorcycles for over thirty-six years. I am a member of the American Motorcycle Association, and I have toured much of the US, New Zealand, Nova Scotia, Scotland, England, France, Italy and Switzerland. I live in the mountains and ride as often as I can now. I often pull into a gas station and smile as I look down at the little kid grinning ear to ear as he tugs his mom towards my bike. I know he will be sitting on a bike before long, just like me.

Chapter One

A Plan is Formed

THERE ARE FEW PLACES ON EARTH THAT CAN LEAVE such a lasting impression of scale and wonder, and the Alps is one of those places.

Right now, though, I'm sat at my desk in damp Manchester. Swirls of steam rise from the surface of a mug of hot tea and it reminds me of another recent drink, not drunk at my desk but enjoyed while sitting on a balcony overlooking a Swiss Alpine view in the morning sunshine.

It's less than a week from my return of the most recent tour and I'm left contemplating how a trip that has been planned over a number of years and months can pass so quickly. Certainly, that's how it feels, but all the photos and the eighteen-plus hours of video footage I returned with tell a different story. A story of a journey that I hope to convey to you in the pages that follow.

It's an account in which we went where we mostly intend to go, we covered numerous miles, we saw many sights and we shared many experiences along the way, and despite my meticulous planning, it was also a journey where I was constantly asked, "Are we doing the Stelvio today?"

The planning started for this trip some years previous. Sat in the mountains of North Carolina, my American friend

Dan expressed a desire to join me on a trip though the French, Swiss and Italian Alps.

Years and several motorcycle tours came and went since that initial conversation. The scale and cost of bringing us all together in Geneva meant that the pipe dream was going to take a number of years to become reality.

In 2017, on a clear summer's evening beneath a blanket of stars, we sat outside our cabin at the base of the Cherohala Skyway. We revisited our previous discussions and were finally able to set a date of 2019 for the trip to finally go ahead.

I rarely mention my travelling companions when I document my travels, although I allude to their presence. Given the character and origin of the group, I want to refer to them in name, since part of the enjoyment of this trip was observing their reaction to the journey, the dramatic roads and immense scale of the scenery.

Dan had been the first person to discuss the possibility of the trip. We have known each over for some time and have rode together many times on the US129 and the surrounding area of the Tail of the Dragon. I had travelled to ride with the group in the US a number of times; I understood the financial commitment of transatlantic travel. This, however, was going to be the trip of a lifetime.

As others became aware of the plan, they also felt that this was a trip that they couldn't miss. And so, with just a target date, the roster increased, with Shane, Eddie and Greg, also from the US, adding themselves to the list.

Shane and Dan would be travelling from their base in Indiana, with Eddie and Greg travelling from North Carolina. They planned to fly to Geneva and rent adventure bikes locally.

The remaining travellers of Nick and Brian were coming from the UK and would again use the Bikeshuttle service that had been used on the previous trip. This allowed us to bring our own motorcycles, with them being transported overnight from Northampton on a lorry as we flew out from Luton to Geneva.

The discovery of Bikeshuttle was a revolution. Not only does it release you from many hours of long and boring French motorway miles, but it puts up to four days of riding back in your budget that can be used exploring the Alps.

The experience leads to a more relaxed outward and inward journey. The two drivers of the lorry that carries the bikes allows them to traverse the distance between depot and hotel overnight, in our case in Thoiry, just outside Geneva. By the time you have enjoyed your breakfast, the bikes are lined up for you, ready to roll out. The homeward journey is just as stress-free.

In the final months before, and with our transport booked, I worked on the routes. Using MyRoute-app, the online route-planning platform, I had mapped out a rough journey that would take us from the two extreme points of our trip and a journey over eight days: Geneva to Geneva.

The most westerly and easterly destinations were the French balcony road the Combe Laval in Vercours and the iconic Stelvio Pass in Italy. My task was to string those two locations together with the best roads I could find, while taking in as many Alpine passes as possible.

I have planned a few tours now and have completed numerous trips that have been subject to a pre-planned route. Additionally, I've had a number of overseas visits that have largely involved riding motorcycles, particularly in the US.

For me, planning is part of the enjoyment of the trip.

There is a lot of information out there on websites, in forums and other media such as podcasts, but I wanted to tell you about my approach to planning. Hopefully you will find this useful if you plan to do the same.

My Approach in Bite-Size Steps

1. How Long Is the Trip

It's important to have a feel for how long the trip will be. This will give you a rough idea of how many miles you will be able to cover. Also consider that time and miles go hand in hand, as I will explain later. My average riding time in a day is around six hours. This may not sound a lot, but if you've chosen the right destination, I guarantee you will have many stops to whip the camera out or just enjoy the views. I also allow time for lunch, and a few refreshment and comfort stops.

2. What Are the Road Conditions and How Many Miles Will You Cover in a Day

The mileage covered in six hours on a motorway will be considerably more than that covered on a mountain pass full of switchback hairpins. If the going is slow you may find that over an average daily ride of six hours your distance may be much lower but no less enjoyable or rewarding. You could find yourself doing 400 miles and in the same period the following day, you may do 150 miles.

3. Don't Be a Slave to the Destination; Enjoy the Ride

You are there to enjoy the ride. There is nothing worse than racing to a destination and missing out on everything in-between. Take your time, look at the scenery, stop for a while, savour it. If you leave yourself some time to relax, you will get so much more out of the trip. If you are going to arrive at your destination early, then do a quick detour and explore. You may look at your planning and think that you haven't covered many miles, or the ride time is only x hours, but trust me on this.

4. How Many People Are on the Trip

Two's company and three's a crowd, as the saying goes. Either way, it comes down to your personal preference and what size of group you normally ride with. Personalities also factor into this, but I find that whatever the number, make sure you are on the same page. Some people want to follow and some people want to be involved in the planning. Whatever you do, agree on the plan before you go. There is nothing worse than a member of the group having their own itinerary. Stay on the same page and stay happy.

5. Start With a Rough Plan; Just the Start and Finish

OK, so now we have the basic pre-requisites and we are ready to start some meaningful planning. Before we continue, the next step is basic, but I find it to be an important foundation. Where does the planning start and where does it end? This is especially important when a group is converging for a trip from a wider area. I usually agree on a meeting point, both in time and location, and agree the finish point where everyone goes their own way. Sounds simple, but there is nothing worse than late arrivals and a sudden early departure requirement that jeopardises your weeks of planning.

6. Use a Decent Mapping Service; BaseCamp If You Must

BaseCamp is a Marmite application, but love it or hate it, it does a job. However, while it is an important tool in processing routes prior to transfer to your GPS (and my reference here is to the Motorrad Navigator), it's not the only option. Personally, I use MyRoute-app. Previously I have written on the benefits of this, but essentially it's the ease that you can define a route, while taking into account essential POI requirements, such as fuel stops, etc.

I pay for a premium subscription, which gives me access to

Google Maps, HERE and TomTom, among others. Typically, I draw my route on either the HERE or Google Maps, mindful of a typical daily distance/ride time, until I've defined a route from start to ultimate finish.

7. Google Is Your Friend

The benefits of using Google though MyRoute-app is that I can see a detailed overview of the areas I am riding through. I can see fuel stops, businesses, potential lunch stops and accommodation. I find that Google can offer me a much greater level of detail than any of the other mapping systems. Additionally, I use Google street view to check out the roads and views. I find this especially useful when I see a side road. Is this a gravel track of no value, or is it a nicely surfaced mountain pass with a vista that can take your breath away? It really gives you the confidence to see that you are taking the right road and not ending up in an industrial park in the middle of nowhere.

8. Google Is Your Enemy (In the Alps, Anyway)

Beware. The flip side of this is in my experience Google is a little too clever for its own good. When planning in advance, Google takes into account current road conditions. Planning a run through the Alps in July and defining a route in November? Forget it. Google expects the roads to be covered in twenty foot of snow and tries to take you a very, *very* long way around.

9. Fine-Tune Your Route

This is the time to visit the forums and ask any questions from people who have ridden in the area. Especially important if you are visiting uncharted territory, and certainly advisable to get the most out of your trip. There is nothing better than prior experience.

10. Group Consensus

Time to take stock of where you are at. If, like me, you are left to do the planning with little interference, then this is the opportunity to get the rest of the party involved. Better that someone mentions that they wanted to visit A or ride road B before you get to the accommodation booking stage.

11. What Accommodation Do You Want

Camping, glamping, B&B or hotel? That's your choice. Personally, I look for a hotel or B&B, although I have been known to glamp or use a hostel (Bramans, France on the last Alps trip; and Applecross, Scotland on the NC500 respectively). Essentially this is defined by how many people you have and what their expectation is. It's worth a discussion before you book accommodation.

12. Divide and Conquer; Where to Stop

OK, so now you have a provisional route. You've got the basics of where you want to visit, and your mileage (or daily ride time) is about right. The next step is to book the accommodation.

I usually follow my route until I have reached the desired daily miles covered, or the riding time taken, whichever comes first. I look for the nearest place name and use a site like Booking.com (other sites are available) to search for local accommodation that is acceptable in appearance and has the right rooms available. It may be that at this stage you need to adjust your route to take into account the location of available places.

Having found the right accommodation, I adjust my mapping software to take into account the location of overnight stop and then repeat the process until I have completed the whole tour. One of the benefits of using a site like Booking.com is that accommodations can be cancelled at no cost anything up to a day before. Useful if you have any mishaps and need to adjust your plans on the fly.

I do know that many people book while on the road. I do see the appeal of this, but for me it's just one more thing to distract me from the tour. The more I can plan ahead, the less I have to think about when I'm on the road.

13. Slice and Dice the Route; Daily Segments

So, we have a route which is notionally divided by overnight stops, but you've mapped out the entire tour as a single journey. It's time to chop those days up. There are many ways to do this depending on what mapping system you are using. I tend to copy the entire route and delete the waypoints from days before and after the one I am focussing on. When I am finished, I make sure that they are nicely titled so I can locate them easily on the GPS. At this stage I always make sure that I change the active map to the native map for the GPS system I'm using. In my case I use HERE for the Motorrad Navigator/Garmin system.

14. BaseCamp: A Necessary Evil

Whether you have used BaseCamp or not, I would suggest its good practice to use it to send your routes to the satnav. I can't speak for other systems, but I have found that while MyRoute-app has plugins to send the route directly, it is advisable to let BaseCamp do a final route calculation using the same map and settings that you have on the device.

You may also want to add further shaping points at this stage to make sure that you stay on track. There are plenty of articles on the Internet and on Garmin's website that go into detail on waypoints, shaping points and manual versus automatic calculation of routes. All I will say is that you should not use automatic calculation or you will lose all those hours of defining the roads you want to ride in-between your start and finish waypoints.

15. Take an Analogue Backup of the Itinerary
My itineraries have been the butt of many jokes (I'm the holiday rep), but for me they are an invaluable backup. I would strongly suggest that you create a document that has your main waypoints listed, prints of the routes and addresses, and booking confirmations of all the accommodation.

16. Research the Local Rules and Packing Requirements
Riding in different territories often comes with different rules and regulations. Research them. All the information is available online and covers the requirements to carry yellow vests, breathalysers, spare bulbs, documentation, first aid kits, reflective stickers on your helmets, use of speed camera arms on satnav devices, use of cameras on bikes, Vignette (road tax) stickers, etc. Many people don't bother with many of the more innocuous requirements, but I would suggest that it would at least be advisable to be aware of them.

17. Sit Back and Enjoy the Ride
I find that the planning is an essential and enjoyable part of the tour. The more I can plan beforehand means the less I have to think about when on the road, and subsequently the more relaxed I will be and the more enjoyment I will get.

All of the above approaches to planning had once again been applied to this trip.

Chapter Two

The Journey Begins

FITTINGLY WE WOULD BE MEETING UP WITH THE American contingent on 4th July in a hotel just over the border from Geneva in Thoiry, France. Their travel plans, however, would have them arrive the day before. Greg and Eddie were taking an internal flight to JFK, a flight to London, and then the short flight over to Geneva. Dan and Shane were departing from Chicago but were then picking up an interconnecting flight in Reykjavik to Geneva.

Back in the UK, my bags were packed, the bike loaded and all pre-flight checks done in triplicate. All that was left to do was wait and follow the social media posts of their journey's start, and subsequently, watch their flights progress on Flightradar24. I was itching to leave and watching them already on the way wasn't helping my impatience.

Greg and Eddie were making good process as I took up my role as UK travel headquarters and command centre (I needed something to pass the time and keep me occupied). It soon became clear that Dan and Shane had a problem. The estimated arrival time at Reykjavik was looking to be ten minutes after the departure of their next flight to Geneva. Not good.

Once they had landed, they were able to update us on the

nature of the delay. The plane from Chicago was apparently too heavy and the delay was caused by having to burn off fuel. I was amazed that this can happen but I've since been reliably informed that it does happen more frequently than you would think. Regardless, someone who calculated the fuel probably would have got an arse-kicking.

Icelandair had already made alternative arrangements and had booked them on a flight to Copenhagen and then on to Geneva. They would be a little late but at least arrive in time to collect their rentals before my arrival and our Friday morning departure on the 5th.

Eddie and Greg, meanwhile, were sailing through Heathrow and subsequently en route for Geneva. Still at home, I joked that the worst-case scenario was that while Shane and Dan were also now heading to Geneva, their luggage wasn't. Sure enough, they arrived at the airport, but their bags were still in Iceland. I hate being right on such an occasion.

Searching for all possibilities of routing the luggage, even to the point of seeing if I could get it over to the UK to get on our flight, I finally gave up and realised that the carrier surely knew baggage logistics better than I could. It was time to see if I could get to sleep, my mind buzzing with the previous events.

It was soon time for my departure. I rolled my bike out of the garage at 6:30am. It was a bright, sunny morning and it looked like it was going to be a fine day. I had spent the last week looking at the weather, from my UK departure and across all the destinations along the route. We were on the back of a heatwave that had baked Europe, but there had been a suggestion of subsequent rain and thunderstorms. Although I had rain gear packed, I was hoping for good weather. I was glad that the forty-degree heat had subsided, but it would have been a shame for Dan, Shane, Eddie and Greg to experience the Alps for the first time with it shrouded in mist and rain clouds.

I rode off my driveway with all the usual sense of excitement and anticipation that I feel on the initiation of a long journey. Meeting up with Nick along the way, we headed south to the Bikeshuttle depot at Northampton where we would meet Brian, who was travelling up from the south. Our route was mainly on fast motorways and it wasn't long before we got to the depot. We quickly checked in and handed the bikes over. Having changed into our casual travelling clothes, loaded the suits and helmets into the Bikeshuttle boxes, we could take time to relax and let them start the overland journey as we flew out to Geneva.

Back in Geneva, the Americans were combining sightseeing with visits to the airport to find out what was happening with their luggage. By the time we had landed and transferred to the hotel at Thoiry, they had since picked up the rental bikes and were waiting to get acquainted with Brian and Nick, whom they had yet to meet.

Our American companions were waiting for us at the hotel reception. As we emerged from the bus, I was greeted with a firm embrace and slap on the back from Dan, Shane, Greg and Eddie. It had been a couple of years since I had last seen them back in the States. In the case of Greg, it had been a couple of years on top of that. It was great to see them again and I quickly turned to introduce Nick and Brian to the group.

I did wonder how the initial meeting would go, but it should have been of no concern. I had stuck them together in a Messenger group and they had been interacting and bonded through the final stages of planning for a couple of months. We were soon in the bar next door, exchanging stories of our inbound travels over beers and a most excellent platter of seafood tapas.

We had, at this point, learnt that the luggage would be coming from Reykjavik on a flight that would not be in Geneva until 1:30pm. Our first destination was the Combe Laval in the Vercours, south of Grenoble. A hasty recalculation of the plan showed the possibility of Dan and Shane taking the fast road south after collecting the lost luggage, while myself, Greg, Nick, Brian and Eddie meandered over to Bonneville and over the Col de la Colombière heading towards La Clusaz and Albertville. This would have us arriving at a point near Grenoble, where we would regroup. Happy that we had a plan, we retired for the night.

Chapter Three

The Long Road to Grenoble

I T   W A S   A   W A R M   N I G H T   A N D   I   A W O K E   S W E A T I N G , despite the air-conditioned hotel room. It was still early, and we were not expecting our bikes until 8am at the earliest. Having dressed and sought out a coffee, we strolled to the rear of the hotel to find that not only were the bikes unloaded, but they had made good time and had arrived at 5am.

We finally had all riders and all bikes together ready for departure. I was on my BMW R1200GS Triple Black, Nick was on his BMW S1000XR and Brian on his BMW K1300S. As for the rentals, Dan was on a BMW R1200GS, and Greg, Shane and Eddie had opted for the BMW 750GS.

The bikes that had been on the Bikeshuttle were brought around the front of the hotel, joining Greg and Eddie, who were still assembling their luggage on the bikes. It was an extremely hot morning and while they continued to load up, we retreated to whatever shade we could find. Dan and Shane were purely observers, unable to partake in any activity until they had been reunited with their luggage at the airport due in later in the afternoon.

I was urging everyone to get loaded and I could see Nick getting impatient. The heat wasn't helping, but Greg and Eddie were used to riding in hot conditions, and while we had been suffering in full riding gear for some time, they went from T-shirt and shorts to fully suited in seconds. We were finally ready to depart. Our efficiency in loading up and getting on the road would have to improve as the week went on. By 9am we rolled out of the hotel gates and headed to downtown Geneva.

Our hotel was in Thoiry, France. But the most direct route would take us over the border into Switzerland and past CERN. This was the home of the Large Hadron Collider, the world's largest and most powerful particle collider and the largest machine in the world. The science people were turning up *to do what they must because they can, for the good of us all (except the ones who are dead)*, I recollected the song *Still Alive* in my head. OK, enough *Portal* references, I had junctions to navigate in a busy Geneva rush hour.

We were initially heading for a Swiss motorway (for expediency) and during the final preparations for our Alps tour, I was wondering whether I needed a 'vignette'. What is a vignette, where would I need one, where could I get one, and why didn't I have one on my last visit to the Alps?

The vignette is a sticker that is purchased and placed on the window of your vehicle. It is a requirement to travel on the Swiss motorways and lasts for twelve months from purchase. Anyone being caught without one will face large on-the-spot fines. That doesn't mean that you will need one to travel on other roads in Switzerland. This is perhaps why I didn't have one last time and avoided any fines.

Prior to my last visit, I knew that there was such thing as a vignette, and I intended to get one if needed. Looking back, I now understand that much of my motorway travel had been through Italy and France. In these countries you do not use a vignette and instead pay a toll. Lots of tolls! When compared to the tolls paid, it looks relatively inexpensive.

Vignettes can be bought at most border crossings, petrol stations, post offices and online. I purchased mine for this year's trip online.

I wanted to have the peace of mind that I had the vignette. This would prevent any delay in having find a fuel station or be fumbling for cash at a border crossing. The cost of the vignette is currently 40 CHF and I paid £32, plus a small handling fee.

The vignette will normally be checked at border crossings, and you will be asked what roads you intend on using. Presumably this is where you will be given an opportunity to buy a sticker if you don't already have one. Hopefully you won't immediately get the Monopoly 'Go to Jail' option and get presented with a 400 CHF fine. I only ever remember going through one manned checkpoint and that was crossing out of Geneva into France. This may have been down to the more scenic routes we selected.

It wasn't long until we reached the main border crossing back into France. A few nervous seconds as we were eyeballed from the manned outposts ensued, but I sailed through with my vignette on display. Not that my sticker mattered now; we had crossed into France, land of the relentless toll booth.

Picking up the A40, we made good progress and reached Bonneville with the intention of finding breakfast. It was 10am and we had been riding for an hour. We were later than expected as we had intended to be away from the hotel at 8am, but regardless, we still needed some refreshment. We pulled into the car park of La Panière for a petit déjeuner.

Eddie had been complaining that his bike was having trouble finding neutral and by the time we pulled up in the car park, he was determined to get it sorted. Being unable to find neutral was frustrating enough but having to hold in the clutch while juggling a payment card at the frequent toll booths wasn't going to be an option. I jumped on his GS and quickly determined that you could only find neutral with the engine off. Clearly there was a problem; he just had to get the rental company to agree.

We sipped our coffee and ate our croissants while Eddie paced around the tables on the phone to the rental company. He described the problem and explained that he had plenty of motorcycle experience; this wasn't his first rodeo. I pulled up the address of our current location on my phone and he tried his best to pronounce the French text before giving up and taking a photo of my screen to send them. He stabbed at his phone before announcing he was putting them on speakerphone, unsuccessfully. Shame, I would have liked to hear the other side of the conversation.

Finally, they reached some level of understanding and agreed to ride out and inspect the bike. Either way, we were losing another rider. Seven had become four, and four became three. We had expected to get lunch at La Clusaz, and assuming he got a speedy resolution to the fault, that would give Eddie the chance to catch up. Meanwhile, Dan and Shane had confirmation that their bags were definitely on the incoming flight and were heading out to the airport.

Leaving Eddie with his malfunctioning GS, I led Greg, Nick and Brian out of the car park with the satnav set on a course for the Col de la Columbière and Le Grand Bornand. The original route had been south from Bonneville on the D12, but at the route-planning stage I noticed that the D4 slightly further to the east was considerably 'wigglier', and a quick look on street view confirmed my suspicions. It was a fantastic road, and gave Greg his first taste of both hairpins and scenery.

We crested the top of the pass and pulled over for a photo opportunity and to get an update on the rest of the party. Dan and Shane had their bags in sight and were speeding through the airport to get back to the hotel and their bikes. Eddie, in the meantime, had been enjoying a farmer's market prior to the arrival of a replacement bike. Unable to find a roadside fix, gone was the 750GS, being replaced with a Triumph Tiger 800.

We were on plan C at this point, but it seemed to be working. Dan and Shane would be right where we needed them near Grenoble and Eddie would be catching us up at La Clusaz, which was only thirty minutes away. Dropping down from Le Grand Bornand, we picked up the D909 that would take us into La Clusaz for lunch. We rode through the village and climbed out on a road that overlooks the centre of town, where we stopped close to a restaurant that we had visited on our last trip.

The sun was high in the sky and the temperature was still climbing, so it was a great relief to find shade and get the jacket off. With liquid refreshment on the way, we scrutinised the menu and checked on everyone's progress. We were using an app called Life360, which was tracking everyone's location. The use of the app was with the intention of hooking back up should someone get lost, but in the current situation it was proving invaluable at timing our convergence. We could see that Dan and Shane were back at the hotel. No doubt they would be loading up the bikes, hoping for a brisk departure and run down to Grenoble. Eddie also looked to be on the move and approaching fast.

The waiter was typically in no hurry and I started to eyeball the time. There was a possibility with people now making progress that we would be the last rolling up at Grenoble. Luckily, we were keeping it simple: pizzas for everyone. We finally caught the eye of the waiter, who strolled over to get our order. We confidently pointed to our selected pizza and were informed that there were no pizzas today! Well, thank you for informing us when you handed us a menu full of pizza options, I thought with frustration. He strolled off again, leaving us to re-examine the menu. After what seemed like an age but was probably just five minutes, he returned to take our alternative selections.

I checked the app again. Dan and Shane had left the hotel and were making good progress. Eddie's location seemed to be where we had left the bikes and I was expecting his face to appear in the restaurant at any moment. Our food arrived, and with no Eddie I again looked at the app to see that he was on the move and had passed the restaurant. As we concluded our lunch and paid the bill, I got a message from Eddie that he had seen the bikes but wasn't sure if they were ours, so had gone on to Flumet. I don't know how many other bikes in La Clusaz there were covered in very recognisable US129 and Cherohala Skyway stickers, but I suppose it's an easy mistake to make. We got back on the road and left La Clusaz behind us.

We rode into Flumet and spotted the Triumph Tiger that had replaced the BMW GS. As we pulled up on the opposite side of the street, an exuberant Eddie appeared, soaked head to toe. He had found an old drinking trough used to refresh the horses in years gone by that had cold water running through it. Not wanting to pass on the opportunity on such a hot day, he had drenched himself in the cool water. Soon we were doing the same. It was like finding an oasis in the desert.

It was still a good run to Grenoble through Albertville, where we picked up the A430 following the Isère river. By the time we picked up the A41, we were making good time, despite the constant disruptions caused by the toll booths. To make matters worse, it was pot luck at each automated toll booth whether they would accept a US card, much to the annoyance of the traffic queued up behind.

North of Grenoble we pulled off what was, by then, the E712 for fuel and refreshment. It had been a long and hot day, which had not been made any easier by the travel disruptions of lost cases, late starts, rearranged routing and bike failures. After filling the bikes with fuel and going into the kiosk to get much-needed water, I emerged to find Dan and Shane stood outside. We had overshot the meeting spot as they were waiting, and they had seen us charge on past. It didn't matter, they had chased us down and we were seven riders again.

While we didn't have to be anywhere by any time, it was now 5pm and we were still two hours off our next destination. The reason we had found ourselves this far south was the Combe Laval balcony road, and it was not an option to not see it. We were all feeling the heat, but we pressed on, and after a few wrong turns in Grenoble, got onto the road that would lead us to what we hoped would be something special. After making the effort, we really wanted it to be special.

The final run south was a long, uneventful road and I did question the logic of the route, given the heat and the time. We were pushing thirty-eight degrees Celsius at this point and I was close to suggesting that we just head back to Grenoble and to our overnight accommodation. We sought shelter at the side of the road and took on liquids. A group decision was made. There was no way that we weren't going to make the Combe Laval after making it this far, but once there we would take the most direct route back to Grenoble and ditch the programmed route. As I finished another bottle of water, I felt I was hitting a second wind. Not wanting to waste it, we got back on the road.

The road was flat. Every so often we caught a glimpse of a rock formation and I was waiting for the satnav to tell me to turn towards it and start to climb. When we finally did turn, the road climbed but not spectacularly so. We were on the

D76 and I knew this was the road, so we pressed on. Then, as the road snaked around, we caught a glimpse of what we had come for through the trees. Majestic steep rock faces bathed in the evening sun, dramatically dropping down to a flat valley floor many, many metres below. This was the Combe Laval and its balcony road that lay ahead of us.

To say that the Combe Laval is impressive is an understatement, and it's hard to convey the scale of the place. Located in the Vercors Massif, the magnificent balcony road is carved directly out of the cliff face. A small wall stands between the narrow road and certain death of a sheer drop of close to 1,000 feet.

We took many photographs and I don't think any of them fully do the place justice, but it was time to experience the road that we had come so far to ride. Everyone with a GoPro checked their battery level and that there was still plenty of space on the memory cards. This was a run that would be captured and replayed on many an occasion. I slung my leg over my GS and led everyone out.

I was mindful of how narrow the road was and if there would be any oncoming traffic. It was getting late and while I'm not sure how busy it can get, on this occasion it seemed that we had the place to ourselves. My focus on what might come around the corner was a welcome distraction, though, and one that stopped me peering over the wall too often.

The main balcony part only runs for a couple of miles and all bikes soon pulled into a lay-by on the far side of the balcony. It was nearly 8pm and the planned route would take another two hours before we saw our hotel. We were all weary and the heat had left us exhausted. As expected, I did a quick check on the most direct route to Grenoble and it showed we could be there in an hour. The route took us back the direction we had come. We didn't need any more encouragement. Back on the bikes, we turned around and rode the Combe Laval again.

We arrived at our hotel, having traversed a busy Grenoble city centre. With the bikes unloaded, I found the access codes to get our room keys. It was late and any hint of hotel staff had disappeared as fast as the light was fading outside. After a most welcome shower, we met outside and tried to formulate a plan to get some food. It was more a case of finding anywhere that was open. What had been a busy city was now more like a ghost town. It was Friday night at 9pm. Where was everyone? If I could offer any advice to any future traveller, it would be to avoid Grenoble.

We did eventually find a bar come betting shop, and nearby, a pizza shop. The heat had got the better of me and I was feeling sick. Skipping the pizza, I tried my best to get some liquid inside me and keep it there. It's a battle I lost, and I unleashed the contents of my stomach in the grid outside the pizza shop. This was another hard lesson learnt. In hot weather, take in liquids little and often. If you feel thirsty, it's probably too late and you are starting to get dehydrated.

I was ready for bed. It was another long ride tomorrow. I'd just have to rest up and sleep this feeling off.

Chapter Four

The Highest Road in the Alps and the St Bernards

WHEN PLANNING THE ROUTE, I KNEW THAT TO MAKE it work, the first two days were going to be long. I don't usually plan to do many miles, going on the principal that it's best to enjoy the journey and not be a slave to the destination. That said, however, much of today's route would be a replay of a previous route but with a couple of hours added on. These two hours would take us from Grenoble to La Norma, where we had stayed on our 2016 outing.

I had started to realise that a larger group is less efficient than my normal size of three or four riders. With seven, there was hidden time that I hadn't taken account of in the route planning. It took longer to saddle up, longer to refuel and longer to take lunch. Every stop incurred a time penalty, but things were improving. Nick, Brian and I emerged from the hotel to find that everyone else was already busy loading up. If it wasn't for us waiting for non-existent hotel staff to check out, we would have had got a swift getaway. As it was, we hung around, waiting for a receptionist to appear, in the end giving up and posting the keys through a deposit box.

Having got out of Grenoble briskly, we made progress on

the main A41/A43. With mountainous areas tantalisingly in the distance, our progress was only interrupted by the occasional toll booth. We were finding our rhythm with the tolls and had worked out what cards worked, and which cards were being rejected by the automated pay points.

As our northerly route arched and headed south once again on the *l'autoroute alpine* towards Saint-Jean-de-Maurienne, I got the signal that some of the bikes that didn't have the range of the 1200GS were on reserve and needed fuel. After a good ten miles or so, I had yet to pick up on an opportunity and my fuel was now getting low. The last thing we needed was another disruption. Today was going to be a day free of delays and the last thing we needed was a bike out of fuel by the side of the road. I started to zoom in and out of the map on the GPS, looking for a fuel symbol and, not finding anything on our direct route, found one just off the autoroute. Turning off, we thankfully found a supermarket with a fuel station forecourt. I'm sure, by this stage, that Brian's K1300S was running on fumes.

Refuelled, we pulled away from the Intermarché Supermarket with a sense of relief, and I tried to steer us back on route. We negotiated numerous small roundabouts while I looked for the road that we were supposed to be on.

In a moment of distraction, confused by the road layout ahead of me and the depiction on the GPS display, I hesitated and studied the map. In that split, a car appeared from my left. Possibly it was going a little too fast; either way I grabbed a handful of brake. My foot, however, didn't react as fast, and by the time my boot planted itself on the road, the bike was already getting the better of me.

I was fully laden with luggage and a full tank of fuel. It was past tipping point and I had little option but to bail from the bike and let the crash bars do what they were there for.

By the time I'd turned around I had two helpers who had quickly dismounted and come to my assistance. The three of us wrestled the bike upright and I inspected the damage. A scuff to the engine bars and hand protectors, but most significantly I'd snapped my brake lever. I've seen a Harley dropped before and a full clutch lever go spinning across the tarmac – game over! Luckily in my case, the GS lever has a weak point designed to snap without losing the whole lever or doing any damage to the master cylinder. At least I still had something to work with. Still, I felt a proper plonker.

We soon reached La Norma and from that point I was on familiar territory. It wouldn't be long until we passed through Bramans and over the head of the SS25 road that runs down Mont Cenis to Susa. It's a fantastic road, but one I couldn't work onto my route this time.

Just before the SS25 junction, the small village of Lanslebourg-Mont-Cenis was our intended stop. We knew a small shop serving coffee with roadside seating. Almost opposite was a patisserie where we could get croissants and pain au chocolat. It was 11:30am and, while not pressed for time, I was over an hour behind where I wanted us to be. There was a lot of road between us and our evening destination of Martigny.

As we left the main strip that formed the village, we didn't get far before we passed a group of bikes travelling the opposite direction, wagging their fingers at us. A hundred yards down the road we found out why. The road was closed, and with no obvious marked diversion. Steel railings blocked our progress. I pulled over to look at my options. I was pretty sure that this was the main and only route out towards the Col de l'Iseran and I had a fear that we would have to take a long detour to Bourg-St-Maurice and over the Petit St Bernard without doing one of the best roads on the route. I soon realised that there was a shorter route that I could see from the head of Mont Cenis that would drop us beyond the obstruction. However, Shane had other plans and had found an even shorter and more direct route.

I became aware of intercom activity between Dan and Shane, and turned to see Shane pop up onto the pavement, circumventing the metal barriers before shooting down the closed road. A minute later, the message came back that he had found a way through. And so, the remaining group of five adventure bikes and a hyper sport tourer followed suit and rode up over the pavement and beyond the road closure.

Fifty yards beyond the initial barriers, we arrived at what would have been the road but was now a deep chasm. Off to the right, however, we caught a glimpse of Shane, who had circumvented the hole by going through a building site. He waved from the other side of a relatively steep valley of rock and dust as he dismantled a barrier. It was all or nothing. Nick led the way, followed by Greg; I was third, but by that time there were thick clouds of dust being kicked up, making it hard to see where we were going. The GS's road tyres grumbled and snaked slightly as they negotiated the loose surface, but I was soon over the brow of the upward climb out of the gorge.

Brian's K1300S didn't find the going as easy as the adventure bikes, and his front wheel squirmed as his rear spun struggling to find any grip. I was sat with Nick and Dan beyond the site, as the others had gone back on foot to give Brian the push that he needed to escape the building site terrain. With a sense of fulfilment and amusement at Brian's misfortune, we now had an unhindered route and put the obstacle behind us.

The D902 started to climb. It was the first real taste for our American travellers of the hairpins that are typical for Alpine passes. I had travelled over the Col de l'Iseran a couple of times prior to this trip and I was looking forward to riding it again, as much to see their reaction as for my own enjoyment.

Shane, Eddie, Greg and Brian had got ahead of myself, Dan and Nick following our off-road building site activities. When we caught up with them after the initial climb, we found Greg and Shane running around taking photos, and Eddie lay on an embankment of lingering snow, making snow angels. The weather was still hot and the sun was beating down on us. As Dan went off exploring, I joined Eddie and sat on the snow. Nick and Brian soon joined us when they realised how good our icy bench was after our time in the saddle.

Shane climbed down from his mini adventure up from the vantage point where he had been taking photos. He was blown away by the scale of the scenery that stretched out in front of us. To be fair, I'd seen it before, but it still gave me the same feeling. I've ridden with my American friends in the US mountains of North Carolina and Tennessee. These mountains were on a different scale, vast and dramatic. The roads just happened to be a bonus. One that we were making the most of and. whether they realised it or not, we were about to press ahead on what was the highest paved pass in the Alps at 2,764m.

It was busy at the top of the pass. It was a Saturday and it appeared that there was a cross-country event. As we sat outside the café come gift shop surrounded by bottles of Hors Piste (a local brew), the occasional participant would run past. They would be greeted with some encouraging clapping as they continued up the mountainside and over the snow. In this warm weather, it was a curious distraction to us, sat around the table in motorcycle gear.

The drop to Val d'Isere is a treat. The road peaks over the

top of the pass and then starts to snake down, cascading from hairpin to hairpin. Soon, way below in the valley, you catch a glimpse of Val d'Isere and ahead over the peaks of the Graian Alps range, Mont Blanc standing at 4,808m, the highest mountain in the Alps. We continued to sweep down the pass and were soon rolling into the resort that had looked so small and distant from our previous vantage point.

The resort was colourful and bustling. Vibrant bunting crisscrossed the road and gave the place a festival feeling. We continued through the resort and out the other side, still on the D902 towards Bourg-St-Maurice. Our journey would now take us around twenty miles onto Séez and a right turn onto the Petit St Bernard.

While the pass is petit in name, it is no less in stature as a road than its Grand St Bernard namesake, perhaps more so. Both times I have taken this road, it has been to climb up its snaking route and frequent switchbacks. It's a fast road and can be attacked more so than many of the tighter hairpins found on the passes. Dan and I broke away from the group, and the pair of 1200GS BMWs thundered up its faultless road surface. Toes of our boots and the occasional peg touched the surface as we attacked the hairpins, grins ear to ear. The perfect road surface that was baking in the sun gave us the confidence to use every part of the tyre and soon we levelled off, and reached the ski resort of La Rosière, with its south-facing views across the valley to Les Arcs.

We enjoyed the views briefly until the other riders caught up, and after an attempted group selfie, we moved on to the resort, pulling up next to a statue of the famous St Bernard dog. There are plenty of decent shops, bars and cafés in the resort, and we were soon filling up on a mass order of burgers and pommes frites. This would be the last opportunity for some French food. We would shortly be crossing into Italy heading toward the Grand St Bernard, at which point we would cross back into Switzerland.

As we crossed the border into Italy, there was a notable change in the road and the street furniture. The road was unbroken, but it now had a different feel, definitely more 'Italian'. Not far from the Italian border, we broke off from the SS26 at La Thuile and onto the SR39 towards Arpy. This was a gem of a road that I was introduced to on my last trip. It would be all too easy to stay on the SS26 and miss this road.

After initially breaking off the SS26, you could be forgiven for thinking you had taken a wrong turn as we travelled through what felt like a small residential area before picking up the SR39 proper. The road opened up to two lanes surrounded by rolling wooded hillside. A few miles further on, the road starts to climb into the fir tree woodland, with the road weaving left and right as you start the seven-kilometre climb up the Colle San Carlo, with an elevation gain over this distance of 530m. The road is very popular with cyclists, featuring in the Giro d'Italia race, and you can often see old mattresses roped to the barriers at the roadside on the hairpins.

The treat, however, is the 10.5 kilometre, 1,049m ascent down to Morgex, with relentless switchbacks through a forest. The fresh pine smell and the shade of the trees a welcome relief from the heat. This pass is to be enjoyed as much as its more well-known counterparts. All too soon the town of Morgex comes into view and the road levels off as you once again approach civilisation.

It was a twenty-minute run from here to Aosta, where we would turn north and pick up the road that ran up to the Grand St Bernard. It was a late Saturday afternoon and our group was being overtaken by many local bikes that had been out for a weekend 'hoon' in the passes and were returning home. I let them pass and I signalled that I would be looking for a refuelling opportunity in Aosta, perhaps the last opportunity before the next pass.

When we found a small fuel station it became evident that we were short in numbers. Greg and Shane, in all the excitement of the local traffic, had picked up the tail of a pack of bikes and had shot ahead without me realising. A quick check of their location showed that they were well on the way. We continued to fill up and I hoped that they picked up the right road to the summit of the Grand St Bernard. If they accidentally peeled off onto the T2 tunnel, they would miss the pass and emerge on the opposite side, beyond Bourg-Saint-Bernard.

We climbed the Grand St Bernard, avoided the junction to the tunnel and arrived at the car park of the Hotel Italia, where we found Greg and Shane. It was early evening, and the souvenir shops and cafés were about to close. As we took in the view and watched the last of the day-trippers disperse, I considered the remainder of the route. It had been a long day, as was expected. There was a couple of planned diversions on my route to Martigny, but given the time, I decided that it would be best to take the most direct course.

As we departed from the Grand St Bernard for Martigny, crossing back into Switzerland, Greg and Shane decided that they would follow my original route that they had programmed in their GPS. This would take them off our direct route at Orsières and towards the pretty town and the Alpine lake of Champex-Lac. We had visited this on a previous trip. A hairpin climb suddenly reveals a small resort with a lake of azure blue. Like a little oasis, the lake hosts fishing and boating activities surrounded by the mountains.

Perhaps in hindsight we should have taken this route, as it wasn't much longer after our arrival at the hotel in Martigny that Greg and Shane too rolled in and offload their bikes. The

Hotel Vatel had a nice, relaxed atmosphere and we were soon showered and enjoying a rather good group meal while we reviewed the day's highlights. I was happy that we had broken the back of the first two days and the additional mileage that had been planned. Not only was the group finding its rhythm, but the days would be more manageable from this point onwards.

Chapter Five

The Grimsel and Furka

THE NEXT MORNING, WE WERE ALL UP IN GOOD TIME, and by 7:30am we were loaded up and ready to go. It was a bright and clear morning. The sun was shining, but this was the first day that there was a real threat of showers.

We departed Martigny in a northerly direction rather than going east and following the valley floor to Brig. I intended to take a less direct but more scenic route through the Alpine valleys of the cheese-making area of the Regional Park Gruyère Pays-d'Enhaut. We would then pick up Interlaken before dropping down towards Obergoms on the Grimsel Pass.

It wasn't long before the sky darkened, and I felt the first few spots of rain hit my visor. My adventure suit is good for a shower, but there is a point where you need to whip out the rain gear. This wasn't the time, but it was getting close. Eddie was the first to bail and he stopped to change much earlier than the rest of us. By the time the remaining group stopped, the rain was about to hit hard. The deluge suddenly hit. Lightning danced through the storm clouds and thunder crackled as we pulled into a deserted self-service forecourt.

We had timed it just right and it was coming down heavy. From our shelter we could see distant blue skies in our direction of travel but overhead it was black and ominous. We gave it a few minutes for the worst to pass before deciding to continue the journey. There was no sign of Eddie, who we supposed had gone an alternative route or was still sheltering from the rain.

By 8:30am, and as we turned towards more interesting roads and landscape, we reached Aigle. The clouds had parted, we had blue skies and as I picked up the turning through the town, I spotted a small roadside café and patisserie. It was a Sunday morning and the few and far between shops were closed. I was a little concerned that our options for this morning's petit déjeuner would be limited. But this café and the weather breaking… well, this was pure divine intervention.

Still a man down (where was Eddie?), we settled into the little café for our morning's refreshments as the American contingent spotted the contents of the patisserie, eyes wide like children outside a candy shop. With noses pressed up against the glass, they eyed the delights within, much to the amusement of the rest of us. As the coffee arrived, so did waves of sweet delicacies which were instantly devoured. I nibbled my croissant.

With clear skies ahead, we were confident that we would have no more need for the wet weather gear, and the pants and jackets were stowed away. As it would turn out, we would not need them again for the rest of the trip.

We left Aigle and picked up the Col du Pillon. Just beyond, we approached a small dwelling by the name of Feutersoey. Spotting a refuelling opportunity, we pulled onto the forecourt and lined up to take turns with the automated pumps.

Having been first up, I finished dispensing fuel, rolled the bike forward to make way for the next participant and heard the unmistakable whine of a Triumph Triple. Eddie rolled up. Realising that he had got ahead of us and had spent his time chatting with the locals, who were probably a little bemused by the American wandering through their quiet village. Fuelled up and regrouped, we continued towards Saanen.

When I had been planning the route, I had spotted a single track just beyond Saanen that took us through a wooded area and then over Alpine pastures. It was a bit of a gamble, but I thought it would be a good option to adventure away from the main roads.

The turn-off for this road was a wickedly acute left turn and, having initially missed it, we did an about turn and picked up the start of the track.

While by no means off-road, the single track was secluded enough to feel that way, and as we passed though the woodland it felt that we were off the beaten track and on a road rarely used, other than by the very occasional agricultural vehicle. The occasional pile of lumber by the side of the track was the only hint of any human activity.

Emerging from the canopy of trees, the track then opened up to a lush, green valley, which was more recognisable as farmland pastures. In the distance, the vista was framed by snow-capped mountains and in this peaceful setting the only noise to be heard, once we had pulled to the side of the track and turned off our engines, was the bells of the grazing cows. The only other sign of life was a farm building perched on the side of the slope that ran to the valley below.

These are the type of places that you hope to find. While this wasn't an adventure across the wilds of an untamed landscape, it was nonetheless an adventure of discovery. In this case, our adventure motorcycles had led us along a small single track that someone travelling in a car would rarely consider finding. No doubt their focus would be on the destination and not the journey itself.

It would have been very easy to stay in this idyllic location for an hour or so, but with so much more to see and places to be, we were back on the bikes and got back on the track that would lead us further down the valley.

Crossing the occasional cattle grid, with its unmistakable vibrating 'brrrp', we reached the valley floor and the road was again lined with trees. Our route would pick up the Jaun Pass and then back to wider two-laned highways towards Spiez. The GPS indicated a left turn and I followed its command. I immediately realised that something was not quite right.

We had accidentally turned into what looked like a residential property, with a steep gravel track leading up to a dwelling ahead of us. Scrambling to get a stable footing, I managed to stop the bike in a location that gave me some chance of turning it around, even if they meant some partial off-road activity over a field of long grass and wildflowers. Having pulled off the move, and with my nose now pointing down the steep path, I slowly rolled past Dan and then Shane. The rest of the group gathered on the road below, having been further back and managing to avoid the wrong turn.

Dan, however, had not been so lucky in his attempt to turn around, and his bike had decided to have an impromptu lie down. Another dropped bike. While I looked for a route to the Jaun Pass without going through private property, the rest went to Dan's aid to lift the prone GS.

Shane had more luck with the lighter 750GS and turned the bike without much trouble. He rode back down the path and out of the driveway. As he joined the group, he lost his footing on the loose gravel and his bike also went over. It clipped a wall and snapped the end of his lever, much the way mine had done the day earlier. A slight smile drew across my face at their misfortune. I was no longer the only person to drop a bike or snap a part off. It gave me some small comfort as I glanced down to my 'shorty' lever that I was now getting used to.

As we composed ourselves and continued to study the map, the property owner emerged from the drive in his car. As he passed, with his window open, he indicated that we would find a way around further down the road. It was obvious that we were not the first up his drive, nor would we be the last. I was unsure if the unsolicited visits amused or annoyed him. He had remained very matter of fact in offering the information.

As indicated, after a short ride down the road, we emerged from the single track onto a junction signposted to indicate that this was the Jaun Pass. I was pleased to be back on track so quickly.

It may seem easy to jump on a motorcycle and ride off on an adventure. For some I'm sure that this is true. I know that there are many who embark on a journey with not much more than a basic desire to explore unknown roads and don't think about where they will be or where they will stay until they get there. Wherever there may be. I, however, had meticulously planned our route. If it felt to my travelling companions that we were accidentally discovering the places that we were travelling through, then this was my intent. In reality, I was always running to a schedule.

What hadn't been planned, and something I was learning on the fly as the trip progressed, was when and where to stop for lunch. It's easy with a small group of three or four, but with this extended group of seven it took a little more thought. I hadn't always got it right over the last couple of days, but I was now being a little more vigilant to the group dynamic. With this in mind, I was looking at the clock and as we approached Lake Thun, we were firmly in the 'window' and I was starting to scan for opportunities.

As we dropped down through Spiez, we caught a glimpse of Lake Thun, and this gave me the opportunity to pull to the side of the road and Google up some options while the group enjoyed the crystal-clear waters of the lake. There were paddle boats, sail boats and what appeared to be a cruise ship enjoying the waters. The sun was high in the sky and its light was shimmering from the turquoise blue waters as I took shelter in the shade of the trees lining the lakeside.

With the group enjoying the view across the lake, it would be a shame to cut short their enjoyment, and my map was telling me that there was a lakeside Italian restaurant (Lido da Elio) only a short ride away. It was 12:35pm and I was satisfied that I was fulfilling my role as tour guide and leader. I think Eddie, who had previously been most vocal about his food, was also especially pleased.

We found the restaurant where it had been indicated on the map. Its large parking area was a bonus as the bikes rode in and parked up. The seating area was overlooking the shores of Lake Thun and the shaded space gave welcome relief from what now turned out to be a very warm day.

We finished lunch and departed, putting the shores of Lake Thun behind us, passing through Interlaken, and replacing them with the shores of the just-as-pretty Lake Brienz, with its similar turquoise waters.

At Innertkirchen, we picked up the junction and sign that we were approaching Grimsel. It had been a great run so far: everyone had enjoyed the roads and the varying scenery, they had been fed and watered in good time, and I was really pleased with the route I had picked. This run was so much better than the Martigny to Brig run that had been on my previous visit.

As we started the run up towards the Grimsel Pass, I was in my comfort zone of group leader and master of the GPS route. So much so that I was slightly taken unawares when an S1000XR shot past me, but rather than being ridden by Nick, perched in the saddle was Eddie. Following lunch, they had decided to try each other's bikes and Eddie was getting a taste of the BMW power unit in the XR.

I picked up the pace and stuck with Eddie, knowing that the group behind me would follow suit or hang back and enjoy the view. No-one would get lost or take a wrong turn. There was only one road, and this was a one-way trip up the Grimsel.

We soon approached and pulled up alongside the Räterichsbodensee, which is one of the lakes on the pass prior to the dammed lake of Grimselsee. The waters of the lake, as are many of the rivers in Switzerland, are a strange green/grey, and it gives a slightly surreal landscape against the mountainous rock faces rising from the water.

The roadside snow that had yet to thaw increased as we approached the top of the Grimsel and reminded everyone that after our travels along the lakeside earlier, we were again at a considerably higher altitude. The Grimsel Pass has an elevation of 2,164m, but we were heading to the Furka Pass that rose higher to 2,429m. It was considerably cooler and there was a slight drizzle of rain in the air as we reached the top of the pass and entered the Hotel Alpenrösli for a coffee and the obligatory trophy sticker. Dan, Shane, Greg and Eddie were collecting the pass sticker and placing them on their helmets. I had the advantage of being on my own bike, so added it to my tally on my panniers. They were at this point starting to look like fighter pilots, with a considerable number of 'kills' on display. Many more were to come, with the Furka Pass next.

The Furka Pass is a particular favourite and has the notoriety of featuring in the opening scenes of the James Bond 007 film *Goldfinger*. James races in his Aston Martin DB5 from the iconic Hotel Belvédère chasing the female assassin in her white Mustang before shredding her tyres with his wheel-destroying spikes. The road is very distinguishable in the film, although its surface is much more recognisable now as a road rather than the dusty surface near the Hotel Belvédère as seen in the film.

Dropping down from the Grimsel to Gletch, you take a left turn and pick up the leading run to the Furka before seeing the road wind back and forth up the side of the mountain ahead of you. High up in the distance sits the aforementioned hotel.

The Gletch side of the Furka enjoys a good wide carriageway that encourages you to breeze past any slower vehicles that threaten to obstruct your enjoyment of the climb up the many hairpins. By the first switchback, I'd despatched a number of cars and coaches, with plenty of room for the rest of the group to follow suit and filter in behind me.

Some of the passes in the Alps are quite narrow and you often are looking for oncoming traffic, or rather the lack of it, so that you can use the full width to negotiate the turn. The Furka, however, has two ample lanes on its hairpins and I was enjoying the sweeping left-hand curves as we ascended.

The right-hand switchbacks are always a little tighter due to their decreased radius and are taken slower. The torquey GS boxer engine, however, just ate these up. Swinging around in second gear, scrubbing off speed to the point where it felt the bike could just lay down, then opening the throttle to slingshot the bike back upright, often lifting the front wheel slightly. This is why we love the Alpine passes.

I swung into the parking area opposite the hotel and close to the summit and was quickly joined by the rest of the group. In addition to the usual gift shop and refreshment bars, visitors can take a walk to the Rhone Glacier Ice Grotto. Greg and Nick did just this as I went through the shop and onto the rear terrace to enjoy the views of the road that we had just climbed up.

As Shane, Brian and Dan took their photos of the vista

and the waters cascading down from the glacier to the valley floor below, Eddie, meanwhile, was in the gift shop, trying to buy merchandise with the wrong currency and arguing the toss over the value of his dollars. I had no such problem and took my Swiss Francs to the stall outside to get some refreshment. The water was refreshing; the price wasn't. It's to be expected that the prices in Switzerland are on the high side, but I'd just paid 15 CHF (around £13) for three bottles of water! I was the captive audience and my thirst was my undoing. I justified my purchase, telling myself that it was better than dehydration.

While everyone finished their sightseeing activities, I hooked up with Shane by the bikes and indicated that I was going to swing 100 yards up the road beyond the hotel to a pull-off area that enjoyed a clearer view of both the passes and the valley to get some photos. Not long after getting my phone out to get some shots, the rest of the group joined me. From this vantage point you can get a clear view of the Grimsel and the Furka crossing the valley floor and you could appreciate the scale of the two passes. A steady stream of cars and bikes continued to wind around their many bends and curves.

The run down the Furka to Andermatt is the stretch that features in the James Bond chase and we took a brisk run down, picking off whatever traffic got in our way. The absence of any form of substantial barrier a constant reminder not to overcook any manoeuvre as certain oblivion beckoned. The view on this side of the pass was not as dramatic as from where we had come, but the road was just as exhilarating. Before long, the road levelled and we rolled into Hospental.

We approached Andermatt and would not be far off our overnight stop of Curaglia. I had initially intended to stay in Andermatt. It's a very pretty and typically Swiss town of wooden structures. With plenty of bars and shops, it is very popular with motorcyclists sitting central to many of the Swiss passes.

We were all ready for fuel and, having previous experience of the town, I knew exactly where we could fill up. Crossing the roundabout at the base of the Oberalp Pass, I guided the group into the small filling station just off the cobbled street.

Will the bikes fuelled, we rolled back onto the roundabout and onto the Oberalp Pass that immediately starts to throw switchbacks at you as you climb out of Andermatt. There was a slight amount of rain in the air; nothing that would influence our choice of riding gear, but with bright sunshine we were graced with the most spectacular rainbow. Its colours were bright and vivid, and unlike the faint rainbows you see from far away, this felt in touching distance. Fighting the temptation to stop and have a look if this pot of gold really did exist, I reached to the camera on the front of the bike in a vain attempt to capture it. I'd been running the camera over the Furka and the Grimsel and alas, the battery was dead. This rainbow would have to remain seen by my eyes only.

I had never travelled further east in Switzerland than Andermatt and I was in new territory. This was the case for everyone, except Brian, who had previously reached the Stelvio on a previous trip, although in his case he had approached it from Italy and the south.

At Desentis/Müstair we turned south onto the Lukmanier Pass for the short distance to Curaglia. As we approached the village, the satnav told me to turn right into a side street. From my understanding of the hotel's location, this was entirely expected, but I soon emerged from the side street to a green valley stretching out before me. This was not expected. Surely I'd missed the hotel and it was one of the buildings that we had just passed?

Looking at the screen, I could see that the route was telling me to cross the valley floor and go up a winding, climbing track to a group of dwellings on the other side. A hesitation of self-doubt came over me briefly, but I knew from the time spent crafting the route that each destination was programmed in with the exact hotel address. I could see the partial address on the satnav screen. This must be right. I went with it.

The road was quite steep, and I hoped I had seen correctly that it reached the buildings on the far side. I hoped that the road wouldn't suddenly turn from single track, to gravel track and then to field, but luckily it carried on. Coming around the final bend, I could see that it ran all the way to the destination and on the final climb and hairpin, I looked up and caught a glimpse of the hotel sign. The curiously named 'Hotel Cuntera'. We squeezed our bikes into the small drive and looked back across the impressive valley view to the village of Curaglia.

Introducing myself at the hotel reception, I was greeted by the owner, a lovely lady who informed me that she had no à la carte menu in English, but if we were able to offload the bikes and be ready in twenty minutes or so, she would prepare us all a special meal. The hotel was the only place on offer, so I accepted the proposal and, after dumping my bags, informed everyone else.

We were soon seated around a table in a large conservatory with large glass windows overlooking an impressive view of the valley. It was a peaceful location and a small number of other elderly guests were also seated in the dining area. I did feel slightly sorry that our large, and often loud, group had disturbed their peace. After a good day's ride, we were in high spirits and it wasn't long before the food was arriving at the table. True to our host's words, we were treated to various dishes of hearty local food that was devoured with relish. The food was washed down with a few cool beers, and the drinking and conversations went on into the evening. Only when the lights went off in the bar did we consider the time, which indicated we should retire for the night.

Chapter Six

Cobbles, Hairpins, Forests and Rivers

LOOKING OUT OF THE WINDOW THE FOLLOWING morning revealed a few low-laying clouds that had descended into the valley. It was a fresh but otherwise dry morning as I retrieved my boots that had been banished to the balcony for a good airing after a few warm and sweaty days. Given the excellent hospitality that had been extended to us the previous night, we opted to take breakfast at the hotel. It was the usual spread of breads, croissants, cereal, cheese and cold meats. I was starting to crave some bacon and eggs, though. I think, similarly, the Americans would have been dreaming of waffles and pancakes or biscuits and gravy.

We left Hotel Cuntera behind us and were weaving back down the winding road to Curaglia, returning to the Lukmanier Pass. Making good progress through Medel, we only stopped briefly at the Arch dam Santa Maria on the Lukmanier Pass before hitting the most southerly point of the days route at Lumino and swinging around north heading for the Mesocco.

As we rolled into Mesocco, the road surface changed to cobbles and the narrow street was lined by three-storey dwellings. Finding an appropriate place to park up on the thoroughfare that was offering little in the way of parking opportunity, we backtracked on foot a short distance to a café we had just passed for some refreshment. There were a few locals outside finishing their game of cards, who then finished their drinks and shuffled off as the group gathered up the other tables and chairs by the side of the street.

The usual array of cappuccinos and espressos arrived together with a large bowl of croissants, which disappeared within minutes as seven hungry travellers grabbed what they could. It had only been three hours since breakfast, but our appetites were insatiable. It must have been the clean Alpine air.

Soon we were back on the road and twisting back and forth on the fir tree-lined road as it climbed ever upward towards the San Bernardino Pass. As we got higher, the trees gave way to a more rugged landscape of rocks, shrubs and wildflowers by the roadside as the peaks of the surrounding mountains came into view.

At 2,066m, we reached the top of the pass and pulled into the parking area of the rustic but functional Ristorante Ospizio S. Bernardino. We weren't alone, and many other travellers and motorcyclists were milling around, either getting refreshments or looking for a photograph near the small lake at the roadside. A small rocky outcrop sat at the centre and protruding from it was a solitary flagpole with a Swiss flag flapping in the breeze.

We started our descent from the San Bernardino's summit, winding down the mountainside until we hit the valley floor at Hinterrhein. Wanting to avoid the two-lane E13, we picked up the more picturesque and sedate road that runs parallel with it at Splügen. We would return and travel the Splügen Pass in the days to come, but for now we continued through the village and past the signs pointing to its pass of the same name.

As we passed the Sufnersee reservoir between Splügen and Sufers on the Hinterrhein river, our route took us into the forest. It was a welcome change of scenery from the dramatic landscapes of the mountains. It felt peaceful, secluded and more intimate.

As we followed the river, I spotted a small wooden suspension bridge and pulled to the side of the road, the group tucking in behind me. We got off the bikes for a closer look. A sign informed us, "*DANGER! Do not stay in the riverbed! The hydroelectric plants may cause sudden flooding at any time; even in good weather conditions!*" Exciting!

Having been alerted to the imminent danger, we filed across the bridge until the predictable urge to rock and bounce the bridge came to everyone simultaneously. The bridge swung and bucked and after a minute of no-one falling to their doom, we decided that we would give up and find other hazards, perhaps on the forewarned riverbed.

The rocks of the riverbed were bright grey and smooth from many years of erosion caused by the water rushing over its surface. A small amount of water flowed, but after ten minutes of exploring we decided that we wouldn't be witnessing the spectacle of sudden flooding today.

It was 1pm and back at the bikes I had a quick check of the map to see what lunch opportunities we had. I was pleasantly surprised, given the secluded location, that the map showed a restaurant named Rofflaschlucht a little further along the forest road. And so, with anticipation of a meal, we headed for this new destination.

Amidst the fir trees and with a steep vertical backdrop of a rockface, the Rofflaschlucht's bright white and classic Alpine-style facia beckoned at the side of the winding mountain road.

Smoke rose from a wood-fired barbecue truck at the front of the building. Leaving the bikes in the parking area to the side, we took our places in the outdoor seating area, with the smell of the burning wood bratwurst further adding to our appetites.

All the usual suspects were on the menu. Rösti, schnitzel and schweinesteak, but the smell of the barbecue had sealed the deal. It was pretty much *kalbsbratwurst mit pommes frites* for everyone. With the orders in and while waiting for our drinks, Dan took the opportunity to take a stroll down to the Rofla Gorge waterfall to the rear of the hotel. Meanwhile we watched on in anticipation as the kitchen staff emerged to cook our sausages on the barbecue truck.

Fulfilled, we left the hotel and carried on with the journey. We left the forest road behind us and, after a brief detour at Thusis for fuel, we headed east on the Albula Pass and then on towards Davos. Our final destination was less than a couple of hours away and as we arrived in the centre of Davos, having made good time, we took the opportunity to stop for a coffee.

The atmosphere was significantly cooler and there was rain in the air. By no means would it force us to reach for the wet weather gear; in fact, it was a refreshing relief, given the previous hot weather. Certainly for us hardened Brits. Eddie was feeling the cold and was swapping jackets like a model backstage at a fashion show.

We left Davos and picked up the Flüela Pass towards Susch. The road was soon lined by fir trees and we travelled into the unspoilt scenery of the Swiss National Park. The rain had started to come down and the roads were as wet as any we had experienced on the trip. We were close to the day's final destination and there was no desire to stop. Given the conditions, it had not slowed our pace and we devoured the last of the curves on the day's route with vigour.

The rain soon broke, and at the head of the Umbrail Pass, it was not long before we reached the signs of buildings and dwellings signalling our arrival at Val Müstair. Not far into the village, we turned off the main road onto a parallel road that overlooked the UNESCO Biosphere Reserve valley, with hillsides rich and green with fir trees. We reached our accommodation, which was an annex building to the main Hotel Schweizerhof Santa Maria, a historic turn-of-the-century building dating to 1903.

The rain, traffic and differing paces had split the group on the approach to Val Müstair, but soon we had all arrived safely and were unloading the bikes. Nick and I strolled up to the main hotel from the annex to check in and after a confusing interaction and conversation in broken English/German with the hotel owner, finally emerged with the room keys.

Having dumped our luggage in the room and after a quick shower, we were sat outside the main hotel enjoying a beer. We were touring on adventure bikes, living out of our panniers and roll bags with what limited gear we could carry. But this was not a reflection of the accommodation that had been booked and in no way were we wild camping. The hotel offered fine dining in a very classy atmosphere and we were soon looking through a menu of the finest cuisine. We were living the trip to the fullest. We were around the midpoint of the tour. We had covered a lot of ground, rode some fantastic roads and seen the most spectacular scenery. There was still plenty to come.

The following morning greeted us with blue skies and only the slightest wisps of cloud. The hillsides were bathed with sunshine, which only emphasised the scale of the valley and the fir trees high up on top. I enjoyed the crisp mountain air as I carried out the now-familiar ritual of repacking the bike.

I've always found that getting the packing right before

departure helps with the unpacking and repacking on a trip, making it a less stressful experience.

I'm not a fully seasoned pro when it comes to motorcycle touring, but I've got a few trips under my belt. I think that's enough to be able to impart some packing knowledge.

There are a few more considerations when leaving home soil. Even when touring in the UK, it's worth putting a bit of thought into what you are going to carry on the bike. While I have the relative luxury of touring with the GS and a full set of panniers, this wasn't always the case. Many of my early trips were on a sport bike, where you really do have to be frugal with what you take.

The first considerations are: where are you going, for how long and how much can you comfortably carry. There are many luggage options to suit all configurations, but I'd advise that you should be comfortable and not overload yourself. Whether you are using hard panniers, soft satchels, roll bags or rucksacks; once you know your capacity, your planning can start there.

I have stated that while I am not a fair-weather biker, I don't do camping. Maybe in the future this may happen, but for now it's hotels, B&Bs and the occasional hostel. So, for now I make no allowance for the packing and transportation of tents or sleeping bags.

It is all too easy to pack too much, especially when you are unsure what you need. I hope that in sharing what I take it can help you decide your own requirements.

The majority of any trip will see you in your riding gear, and since you will be wearing it, you won't have to worry about packing it. That's the helmet, gloves, jacket, pants and boots sorted.

There are some variables dependant on what ambient temperature you expect. I usually wear an adventure touring

Figure 1: The Bikeshuttle lorry.

Figure 2: The Grand Bornand.

Figure 3: Eddie's water trough.

Figure 4: Regrouping near Grenoble; Dan, Brian, Eddie
and Greg (left to right).

Figure 5: Dan surveys the Combe Laval.

Figure 6: Eddie, Nick, Martin and Dan on the Combe Laval (left to right).

Figure 7: Brian is all smiles before his off-road activity.

Figure 8: On the climb to the Col de L'Iseran.

Figure 9: View from the Petit St Bernard.

Figure 10: Single track on the way to the Jaun Pass.

Figure 11: The shores of Lake Thun.

Figure 12: The Grimsel Pass.

Figure 13: On the Furka Pass looking back to the Grimsel.

Figure 14: Filling up in Andermatt.

Figure 15: Across the valley to Curaglia.

Figure 16: On the climb to the San Bernardino.

Figure 17: The small island and flag at the summit of the
San Bernardino.

Figure 18: The foot of the Stelvio.

Figure 19: The top of the Stelvio, looking at the east side.

Figure 20: The west Stelvio heading to Bormio.

Figure 21: Taking my money!

Figure 22: Tax-free Livingo.

Figure 23: St Moritz.

Figure 24: The 'gondola' at St Moritz.

Figure 25: Shane at the Splügen.

Figure 26: The Verzasca Dam.

Figure 27: The cobbled Tremola.

Figure 28: At the top of the Nufenen Pass.

Figure 29: Sunrise in Bedretto.

Figure 30: The Susten Pass.

Figure 31: The waterfalls of Lauterbrunnen.

Figure 32: Overlooking Grindelwald.

suit (RST Adventure Pro II) and have found that I'm comfortable enough with the liners out. That said, I do tend to run 'hot' and don't mind a bit of cold.

Apart from the obvious underwear considerations (where x pairs of undies are equal to x days of travelling), I get away with a couple of pairs of socks for the evening and a good set of riding socks. OK, so they may get a bit fruity by the end of a tour, but by that stage I'm on the home leg and they are heading for the wash.

I do try and wear a good wicking base layer, although since I pack a fresh T-shirt for each evening, I have the option of riding in that the following day.

One tip I can give is to invest in a set of vacuum bags. I have a set that came with a very small hand pump. The pump is not much different in size to the type that you can use to inflate balloons and takes up very little space. On a longer trip, I can take all of my second week's shirts, underwear and socks with half the normal space taken. I swap over mid-trip and once the dirties are 'compressed', I can pop them back in the roll sack I carry.

In Europe, there are a number of requirements for documentation. I usually have a trip itinerary that has a basic list of the route waypoints, contact details and hotel accommodation confirmations. Additionally, in Europe I carry the V5C logbook and a copy of my insurance details. I'll add my passport to the list, however; it's a given since I would need it to get to the destination anyway. It might only be an issue if you've left it at home and travelled a few hundred miles before reaching for an empty pocket.

You might also want to consider breakdown insurance and travel insurance. For the latter, make sure that you do get a specialist policy, as most standard travel insurance only covers motorcycle use up to 125cc. I use Holiday Safe and have always found them to be very reasonable for the peace of mind they offer.

While on the topic of paper-based items, I will mention maps. I use the GPS and invest a lot of time with the routes that I load on it. However, I do always carry a set of road maps covering the areas that I will be riding. If nothing else, they give you the ability to discuss the day's travel with your companions. At worst case, they are invaluable should the expensive toy curl up its satellite-loving toes.

Mention of the GPS brings us conveniently on to the electronics. It is ever so easy to become a slave to the devices. While I am no purist, I do try and keep things as simple as possible. I do take a GoPro camera and value the footage taken, but I've resisted going down the drone route. The thought of having to charge too many devices seems tedious and an unnecessary distraction.

I've also ditched the camera and iPad. These are taken care of by my phone. All the photos I have taken, and that you may have seen on my posts, have all been taken on the phone.

What this means is that if you can reduce the number of items that need charging, then you reduce the number of leads and chargers you need to pack.

The laws differ in various countries, so I would suggest that you familiarise yourself with the destination. This is not just for the legal requirements, but also to check that there have been no changes to the law.

Generally, to cover these local requirements I carry a breathalyser kit, a hi-vis vest, and a first aid kit. I also carry a pack of reflective stickers for my helmet, although I have never used them.

My last few bikes have had 'GB' on the plate, but if you don't have this, you should get a sticker.

At this stage I'm usually packing the small items, although

no less important. These are items such as basic tools, a torch, sunglasses, ziplock bags (one contains a damp cloth), microfibre cloths, visor cleaner, etc.

One more thing. A pen and notepad. How else would I remember all the details of a trip to allow me to write about it here? I'd recommend something durable that doesn't mind a bit of damp, should you get a soaking. I like to use Field Notes.

You might take more or less than I do. Regardless of what you take, I was always told that if you take it and didn't use it, then you probably didn't need it with you.

Chapter Seven

Yes, We Are Doing the Stelvio Today

ARE WE DOING THE STELVIO TODAY? THIS WAS A question that I'd been asked on numerous occasions over the last few days. I'm not sure if it was through pure ignorance of the itinerary that I'd been working on over the last few months, or whether they could see my visible frustration every time I'd been questioned and were just poking fun. Regardless, the answer today was yes. Yes, this is the day that we would be riding on the famous Stelvio Pass.

We wouldn't, it would turn out, be doing the Umbrail Pass. As I selected the route, the GPS grumbled and made attempts to recalculate the route. In each instance I cancelled it, not wanting to disturb my carefully placed waypoints and shaping points that had been defined in my planning applications.

I finally reverted to my phone and saw what was causing the problem. There was roadworks on the Umbrail Pass that were forcing its closure. Other than the obvious frustration that I would not be able to tick this pass off my list, I was going to have to find an alternative route. This came by the way of a looping route around from Val Müstair to Glorenza and Prato allo Stelvio. This allowed us to pick up Trafoi at the base of the Stelvio.

Trafoi had been on our original route as we had intended to drop down the Umbrail and travel down the Stelvio before turning around there and travelling back up. The detour would not have an impact on time due to the road being faster than if we had ridden the Umbrail and we were doing less of the Stelvio than planned.

As we arrived at Trafoi, we rolled the bikes into a lay-by. This marked the start of the run up the Stelvio Pass. Mountains towered in the distance and the road was about to start snaking around the now-familiar hairpins typical of the passes that had already been ridden.

We started the climb. The gradient and the turns were initially relatively gentle, but as we progressed, they became increasingly demanding. At each turn the switchbacks became tighter as we corkscrewed around each incline, progressively climbing higher and higher.

The roads were lined with stone walls and they gave no comfort or feeling of safety over some of the open passes we had ridden previously and their perilous drops. These walls only served to limit the view around the next bend. As we approached each new turn it was a fresh challenge to crane your neck around early to see around and over the wall in an attempt to see if anything was coming the opposite direction that would hinder your progress.

We had picked a good time to ride up this, the most challenging side of the Stelvio. There was barely any traffic and what we did pass was on the straight that connect the hairpins. At least this allowed us to attack each switchback with as much road surface as was on offer.

The switchbacks kept coming relentlessly... eight, nine, ten... then twenty... then thirty... I think there are forty-eight hairpins as you climb up the eastern ramp to the top and they hit you continually with no respite. But then you catch a glance of the village that sits at 2,757m atop of the pass. An oasis of bratwurst stalls, cafés and numerous shops selling souvenirs to the many tourists, some in cars, some on motorcycles and the mad buggers who ride up on bicycles.

The Stelvio Pass is the highest paved pass in Italy (yes, we were back in Italy) and the second highest in the Alps, just 13m below France's Col de l'Iseran that we had crossed some days earlier. While we had previously been at higher altitudes, the air was noticeable thinner here, and having parked the bike up and headed up to the shops on foot, I could feel myself labouring for breath.

There is no doubt that the Stelvio is well-known; its name has been used on motor vehicles and was once named by *Top Gear* as the 'greatest driving road', although they later decided to give that title to the Transfăgărășan Highway in Romania. I recalled many accounts of people who had offered advice, having previously travelled the pass. Much of this was get to the top (presumably via the Umbrail that had been denied to us), eat a bratwurst, enjoy the view of the eastern road and then continue down the western side.

It was a challenging ride up, which had certainly been made easier by the sparse traffic, but I didn't feel that it wasn't a road I wouldn't want to do again. I just didn't think it was a road I would have liked to have done twice in a day and for that I felt that the revised route had done us a favour.

We opted not to have the bratwursts on offer – we had not long eaten a hearty breakfast at the hotel – but we enjoyed a drink while looking at and taking photos of the road route we had just travelled.

For a small village on top of a high mountain pass, I was surprised to find not only so much activity, but also so many hotels and shops. From the Albergo Ristorante Tibet with its Tibetan-inspired tower on one side, to the turreted Rifugio Garibaldi high above where we sat alongside the sausage-munching travellers.

Having bought our trinkets, gifts and T-shirts, we all returned back to the bikes to experience the western side of the Stelvio.

Dropping down from the summit, we passed the junction where the Umbrail Pass meets the Stelvio, and I resisted the urge to turn onto it and ride whatever short distance was available before the road closure.

The western side of the Stelvio is a much gentler ride but no less enjoyable. The hairpins are sweeping, and you have more time to look out at the view as you see the road snake off into the distance.

Dan had a thing for waterfalls and after the initial descent we approached a solitary Alpine-style bar which Brian had mentioned before we left the summit. Behind it, the waters of the still-melting snow cascaded down the rocks. A small pull-off overlooking the remaining road of the west side of the Stelvio gave us a convenient place to stop briefly.

From our vantage point we could see the waters continue on their journey, carving out a route through steep valley rockfaces, the road running to the left of the valley, and a steady stream of cars, motorcycles, bicycles and cross-country skiers passed our location. The people on rollerskis proved a particular curiosity as they worked their way up and around the hairpins. Undaunted by the scale of the climb in front of them, they made steady progress, gliding forward with each stroke and push of their ski poles.

The road levelled towards the valley floor and once through a single lane tunnel, with traffic lights that seemed to take an age to change their colour and allow us to proceed, we were soon approaching Bormio seeking the Gavia Pass towards Ponte di Legno.

By contrast to many of the places we had travelled though, with the exception of Davos, Bormio was a busy and bustling town. Busy roads and junctions cut through the large buildings either side of the highway, and down at street level the pavements were full of people shopping or sitting outside the many coffee shops.

We exited Bormio and its urban tumult towards Uzza, hindered slightly by an excess of roadworks, dust and machinery. The road beyond was quieter and the increasing amount of green scenery indicated we were once again leaving the built-up areas behind us.

As we passed San Antonio, with its flowered balcony residences, the valley view started to open up ahead of us. Our path was unhindered until we approached a group of officials setting up by the roadside. As we got closer, a barrier was placed across the road and we were gestured to stop.

There was no obvious sign of a problem, and the makeshift shelter with tables and chairs indicated that this was a planned closure and not a response to an accident.

The official walked over from his police car and thrust a sheet of A4 paper our direction. And with no words other than a grunt, walked away, leaving us to study the contents of the document. I couldn't read the Italian text, but I could see from the crudely improvised map a bold line suggesting we take this alternative route. Once I had worked out its orientation relative to our location and what I could see on the GPS on my dash, I ascertained that it was a planned road closure.

The group were hot and obviously frustrated while I studied the options and made adjustments to the route programmed into the satnav. The sun was high in the sky and layers were being removed or zips opened to gain some comfort and relief from the heat. The officials continued to set up their makeshift office and made no attempt to enquire if we understood the information on offer.

Not for the first time today, we were being denied a pass. We would not be travelling on the Gavia Pass. Our route would take us back through the roadworks, back into Bormio and then on a fast but uninspiring road to Tirano, where we would pick up our original path.

Back at Bormio, we negotiated the traffic once again, taking the opportunity to refuel before continuing our forced detour.

The run out of Bormio was an arduous mixture of straight carriageways and long tunnels as we bypassed the much more interesting run of the Gavia that was denied to us. As least it was fast and we made brisk progress.

As we passed through Tirano we returned to our planned route, the GPS suddenly springing into life and giving me voice instructions: "Continue on route." We were coming into the lunch window and spotting a parking area to the side of the road with some welcome shade; I pulled over and came to a halt followed by the rest of the group.

In the shade of the trees there was a trough of running water, and we took the opportunity to remove our riding jackets and douse ourselves with the cool liquid. As I reviewed the map, a Porsche pulled into the parking area, beckoning Greg over. He returned with a garbled message that was obviously lost in translation about someone who had been flashing. Perhaps it wasn't so much that there was a pervert nearby; maybe someone who was feeling as hot as we were and had also removed some garments.

With the detour, we had shortened the distance and taken a faster route, which had left us ahead of schedule. I was looking for a place to stop for lunch, but in doing so I noticed a place that had been suggested to me when planning but I had been unable to string into the route.

Not far off our route to the north was the town of Livingo. I remembered it being spoken of favourably from riders who had visited and stayed frequently, and if that wasn't enough of a reason, Livingo enjoys a special tax status as a duty-free area. That sounded very much to me like a cheap lunch. The trip there and back to our route would take no longer than forty minutes – easily time we had to spare.

With full agreement, we prepared to continue, returning our jackets that had been previously discarded. Dan had dozed off in the shade but soon woke up when kicked, and once I could see that everyone was on their bikes in my mirrors, I rolled over to the parking area's exit.

There was traffic approaching from the left but time for us all to pull out if we were brisk. With a flick of the throttle, I pulled out, making sure that I was fast enough to leave a reasonable gap behind me for everyone to fill.

The road ahead was obscured by a slight chicane which flicked right to left. As I emerged and had a clear view of the road ahead of me, the earlier message made sense. This wasn't a sexual predator. Bollocks, Polizia! Peering from a small size street, our 'flashers' were two guys and a speed gun, and we'd been done!

Fifty yards up on the right, a row of orange and white patrol cars sat in a parking bay. Trying my best to look all unconcerned, I still harboured the hope that we had got away with it. We weren't ripping it up, and look, we were on sensible adventure bikes, not sport bikes. Hopes dissolved and stomachs sunk as he waved us in. We were literally a kilometre back into Switzerland from crossing an invisible border from Italy and we'd been given the full welcoming party.

The usual interrogations followed. Licence, passport and vehicle registration documents were handed over for scrutiny. Meanwhile, Nick was getting questioned about his spare glasses, being a contacts wearer, and Brian was getting the same treatment. With a puzzled expression, Brian protested his innocence at not having a spare pair of spectacles on the basis that he doesn't have contact lenses, nor had he ever worn glasses. At this point, the officer was having none of his pleas and just proceeded to explain that his driving licence indicated otherwise. As if the DVLA down in Swansea could never make a mistake? Ultimately the officer gave up, and without any evidence that Brian had contacts, glasses or spare glasses on his person, gave him a firm warning to get his records put straight on return to the UK.

Having been stripped of my documents, I stood by my bike, trying to look as inoffensive and innocent as possible, as my judge, jury and executioner returned. He produced his official chart and then drew my attention to some sums that he had written down in his pad. His calculations showed my speed, minus the acceptable tolerance, which equated to my speed being 11kmph over the stated limit. Drawing my attention back to the chart, he revealed that this would be a 300 CHF fine. I was impressed that he managed to keep a straight face. Maybe this wasn't the first time he'd delivered this punchline.

It was at this point we were informed that it would be the lead rider and the last rider of the group who would be fined. The last rider was Eddie; this would be fun. I looked over in Eddie's direction and his lawyer alter ego had kicked in as he was trying every trick to get off. The officer just carried about his business. This was the Swiss Polizia Eddie, not some North Carolina state trooper. Bend over, take it!

Realising they were off the hook, Dan, Shane and Greg

were having a laugh with good cop as my bad cop lead me to the patrol car to flash my plastic at his card machine. There is something sinister about paying a roadside fine in cash; there is something even more cynical about having to pay via the card machine they were carrying. Reunited with my documents, I returned to the group, still laughing and joking with the good guy.

The fine stung, but like ripping off a plaster it was over, and I put the pain behind me. I gingerly lead the group out of the lay-by, and short shifting, rode away as slow as possible. We were very careful to observe the posted speed after the encounter. At least for a few miles, anyway.

We picked up the Bernina Pass, which helped take my mind of our brush with plod and picked up the turning to our revised waypoint. Crossing back over the border into Italy, we entered Livingo. A wide-open valley with rolling hillside either side, covered in thick fir trees. Cows grazed in the pastures at the side of the road as we approached the town and pulled into an ample-sized car park opposite a Ristorante Pizzeria Whiskeria (should you have ever wondered if such a thing could exist).

We got seated as Greg and Shane bounced into the whiskey shop. Kids in a sweet shop again. They emerged some minutes later with their samples in tumblers. I'd had too many encounters with the law today; just a Coke for me, thanks. After some rather good pizzas, the expectedly affordable bill (duty-free and cheaper Italian prices) was paid, and we left Livingo. It had been the briefest of visits but no less enjoyable. I suspect I would have enjoyed it all the more should I have been in the market for a reasonably priced bottle of Scotch.

As expected, it was only a short ride back over the border and back onto the route and the remaining stretch of the

Bernina Pass. It was a fine afternoon and the voracious heat from earlier had subsided to a much more agreeable level. I settled down and let the big GS do what it does best as we cruised onwards towards St Moritz.

St Moritz is a luxury and iconic ski resort and we were very much looking forward to the glamorous surroundings. As we approached, the late afternoon sun was shimmering off its splendid lake that freezes over in the winter to host polo, cricket and even horse racing on ice.

We circled the town and found a place where we could leave the bikes while we could stroll to the well-groomed shores that surround the lake. Glamorous buildings decorated the hillside opposite with overnight accommodation prices that, I'm sure, far exceed our daily budget if not the total price for the trip.

Further along the shore, we spotted a gondola that looked misplaced and would have been more at home suspended high above the buildings opposite. On closer inspection, we found that it had been converted into a makeshift bar. Stool, tables and relaxed seating were scattered around the grassy apron in front of the structure.

We entered the relatively small silver cocoon, much resembling a caravan in its grounded location. Only the suspension work adorning its roof gave away its original purpose; that and a big sign saying 'Gondola'. Having ordered a round of drinks, our attention was drawn to a stump of wood in the centre of the bar area.

Shane immediately recognised it as a drinking game that he had seen previously, *Hammerschlagen* if played with a hammer; *Nailspielen* if played with an axe. The game is typically played with a ball-peen hammer and a large cross section of soft hardwood as we were seeing in front of us. The aim being to take turns hitting your nail with the small end of the hammer. The winner is the person who first sinks their nail; the loser buys the drinks.

Having gained permission to embark on what was expected to be a rowdy game, the hammer and nails were located, and the players nail arranged around the stump. Shane, Eddie, Nick, Brian, Greg and Dan surrounded the playing area and prepared for the gladiatorial show down.

Shane was first up and, having had a few throws of the hammer to gauge its balance and weight, spun the hammer in the air. He caught the handle and brought it down with a thwack, completely missing the nail and splitting the stump. The hammer passed to Eddie. A few test spins of the hammer, *whack*. He missed the nail, again hitting the stump. The hammer was passed player to player and after the first round, not one nail had been hit. This was going to be a long game.

Finally, some blows were landed on the nails and they started their slow journey into the stump. I'd seen enough and, fearing that the hammer that was being tossed around would be more likely to hit my foot than the nail, took my drink to sit outside and enjoy the view across the lake.

We left St Moritz with what would be a short run of around an hour to our day's destination of Prata Camportaccio that lay back over the border in Italy. Passing Lake Silvaplana, then Lake Sils to our left, we soon approached Maloja.

There had been a number of lesser passes that had turned up on the route that had gone unlisted on the itinerary that we were following. The Maloja Pass was one of them. Joining the Swiss canton of Graubünden with the Swiss/Italian valley of Val Bregaglia, I approached it completely unaware of its existence. Nestled in the side of a steep and unclimbable slope, it winds down with numerous sharp turns. The rate of descent and the frequency of the switchbacks gives you an impressive view of the roads layout below you, carving its way to the bottom.

When you find such carefully crafted roads like this, with the Alpine mountain peaks majestic against blue skies, dropping down to lush valleys of pine forest and green pasture, and pristine turquoise lakes, it's hard not to appreciate why the Alps is one of the greatest motorcycling destinations.

We were now on the final run into Prata Camportaccio. I knew nothing of it as a destination and its selection was purely one of it being in the right place and the right time on the route. An indicated right turn on the satnav lead us onto a side street, and right in front of us our hotel for the night.

We rode to the rear of the hotel to a nicely paved area of ample size for all seven motorcycles and as the sound of the engines stopped one by one, we dismounted and started the evening ritual of removing our luggage.

Our hotel, the Agriturismo Al Palaz, describes itself as an eco-friendly property that produces its own wine, fruit and vegetables, as well as different types of jams. It is set in San Cassiano Valchiavenna, 3.1 miles from Chiavenna. Regardless of this, their postal address and the route in my itinerary said Prata Camportaccio, and I'd only just got used to getting my tongue around the name with my finest Italian accent when asked about the destination.

We got the keys, and as everyone except Nick disappeared into the clean and modern hotel, I remained outside with Nick, sitting in the shade offered by a canopy. The only other person there was a middle-aged man who was finishing a beer in the warmth of the early evening sun getting ever lower in the sky.

We would later get chatting with the guy and learnt that he had ridden with a group of motorcyclists from Germany, but his bike had broken down. He had remained back at the hotel while the locals tried to attempt a fix; his companions had continued on their way. I assume they thought he would catch up, but almost a week had gone by and without successful repair, he was now waiting for recovery.

With the exception of Eddie's gearbox issues which forced the change to the Triumph Tiger 800, the bikes were without issue. The other two BMW F750GSs of Shane and Greg were running fine, with the exception of a snapped lever, as was the other rental, Dan's BMW R1200GS. Brian was still happily cruising on the K1300S, despite having to mix it up with the adventure bikes on some less than suitable roads. My R1200GS was behaving itself, despite a glitch on the GPS that caused it to occasionally reboot, strangely only in France. Nick's S1000XR was also running fine, but Nick was having his head turned by the GS.

I could see by Nick's body language, the odd hints in conversation and his willingness to let Dan ride the XR and he take the GS, that his time with this model was coming to an end. He'd had two XRs, with his first being wrote off in a shunt. It's a great bike that I fully appreciated, having been an owner of a BMW S1000RR superbike. This was essentially the same engine with different tuning and put in an adventure package, but the 'do it all' flexibility and torque of the boxer twin was in its element on this type of ride.

We took our gear to the room, and I sat on the balcony overlooking a grassy agricultural valley surrounded by mountainous areas either side, covered in green vegetation with only the top third exposed rock formation. A light veil of cloud had rolled in and it was comfortably cooler. When my turn came to use the bathroom, I quickly showered and, once dressed, went to find everyone else to see what options we had for evening meal.

I found them in a seating room downstairs behind the

reception. A number of comfortable recliners and sofas were arranged on the tiled flooring. The room adjoined the kitchen and dining area, and while the kitchen staff happily served bottled beer on request, there was no sign of being able to eat there tonight.

I returned to the seating area with my beer to find that the hotel dog, a small, elderly mongrel of sorts, had taken up a chair. I offered a hand of friendship to be greeted with a snarl and bared teeth. I retracted my offer and went to finish my drink on the opposite side of the room. Luckily the rest of the hotel's occupants were more agreeable and approachable.

Greg had enquired on reception and been informed that there was a restaurant a few hundred yards down the road. Looking around the room I realised we were one short. "Where's Eddie?" I enquired. Greg then informed us that no sooner had we unloaded the bags from the bikes that Eddie had gone down to the local supermarket and bought food. Furthermore, this pre-prepared ready meal had been sat in the sink while he had been trying to use the bathroom, as Eddie attempted to heat the dish in hot water. Maybe he was looking for the full adventure experience. We left him seeking a more 'civilised' dining experience.

As stated, there was a restaurant which we reached after a short stroll through residential back streets. A relatively smart-looking Italian restaurant up a flight of stairs. On entry, we paused with the expectation of being asked for our numbers and taken to a table. The restaurant was busy, but not overly so. The waiters and bar staff went about their business, so we strolled further into the establishment and found an empty table on the open balcony area to the rear.

The clouds that had rolled in were carrying some rain and we felt the occasional spot. Looking around, there didn't seem anywhere else available under the awning of the main balcony area. Perhaps that's why they were reluctant to seat us here. By reluctant I mean completely ignored. They had turned it into an art form. Despite walking past the six of us desperately trying to catch eye contact, they maintained their rigid forward gaze as if were invisible. I could have been dancing naked on the table and while the other diners would have been covering the eyes of their children, the waiters and waitresses would still not have looked in our direction.

After an initial fear of a shower, the clouds were now parting and perhaps the low sun that was now peeking through the clouds illuminated us and alerted the staff to our presence. After what seemed like an age, we were taken unawares by a waitress who thrust menus in our direction. I should not have been surprised to find an Italian menu in an Italian restaurant in Italy. I stumbled around the foreign text and picked a recognisably safe option of carbonara. I sipped on a glass of wine while we shared photos and stories of the day's ride, the sun now lowering behind the mountains and causing the remaining clouds to glow pink and orange.

Chapter Eight

More James Bond?

THE MORNING WAS FRESH AND COOL, BUT THE SKY was a clear blue with wisps of white that I wouldn't even describe as clouds. It would soon warm up, so taking the opportunity to throw the bags on the bike, we loaded up before going back in for breakfast.

There was a large spread of the usual continental cheese and meats. Also on offer was a large array of cakes and other delicacies, much to the delight of Dan, Greg and Shane. How they had not put on any number of pounds in weight was a mystery. I was more interested in the homemade jam which they had claimed was from fruit that they had also grown themselves. Seeing as I missed out on their homemade wine, I was going to enjoy this breakfast.

The day's route would take us initially up the Splügen Pass that we had skimmed some days earlier and have us partially retrace our steps in reverse on our way through Biasca where we had passed on our way down from Curaglia. From there we would pick up the road to Airolo.

The route on the GPS led out of the hotel and towards Prata Camportaccio on single track with worked farmland either side of the road. We soon picked up the main road and at Chiavenna we took the road that would lead us to the Splügen Pass.

I had been looking forward to the Splügen and had photos on my phone that I had saved of the picturesque balconies over the road. Prior to our departure, I had often shown people this picture along with others such as the Combe Laval to explain where we were going and what we would see.

The road started to gently climb through hairpins and tunnels but not the quaint structures yet. These were newer, and built of rock and concrete. We carried on and I was slightly puzzled as to why I didn't recognise my surroundings in comparison to the photos I had seen. Surely they had not replaced the balconies?

The road levelled off alongside the dammed Lago di Montespluga and by the water's edge we stopped for a break. This gave me the opportunity to check the location of the road that I was so familiar with from the picture on my phone. Zooming in on the map, I realised the mistake. Stupid! It was a mistake that had been made many months earlier. Just beyond Corti, the road splits. My route had taken us off the SS36 and onto the newer SP1 (also signposted as the Splügen Pass). It was a longer route of three kilometres more, but while faster, it removed the road that I had been so looking forward to taking. I was obviously disappointed, but, on the upside, I don't think anyone else had noticed.

We were ready for a coffee, and the little village of Montespluga looked like a conveniently close possibility. As we turned into the village we found them resurfacing the road and we were quickly directed around the works, bypassing the only café in town. I decided to press on to Splügen, where we would have plenty of other opportunities.

The descent down to Splügen takes the form of a sprawling set of curves and hairpins. The hairpins have ample depth to swing into decisively and the open nature of the vista gives a confidence-inspiring overview of any other traffic that might be travelling towards the switchback you are about to attack. This was an enjoyable road which gave me a rare opportunity to see the rest of the group without using mirrors as I snaked in the opposite direction to those behind me, having rounded a hairpin.

We took our final curve, which straightened out with a direct view of Splügen before us. After a brief hop off the bike to allow Shane to get a picture he'd requested with the Splügen road sign, we parked the bikes and strolled over the bridge. The shallow clear water running over the rocky bed the only noise on this otherwise-peaceful morning. We settled outside the typically Alpine Hotel Suretta on the opposite side of the road from the bridge and ordered our coffee while we enjoyed the pristine surroundings and scenic cobbled streets in front of us.

As we departed, I noticed that Nick and Dan had swapped again, with Nick preferring the more relaxed 1200GS. He'd soon get a chance to get the best out of the GS as we started our climb from the valley floor up the San Bernardino Pass. Sixteen hairpins later, we gazed down to the road far below from whence we had come.

It was only a few smaller hairpins now to the summit of the pass, but as Shane approached one of the remaining switchbacks, a large truck, that had just passed the lead riders, arrived at precisely the same moment. He hit the front brake hard on the apex of the bend; the front washed. The camber of the road, together with his short legs, meant the bike was going down. He slid for a couple of metres and as Dan pulled up behind the prone bike, Shane dusted himself off, picked the GS up and pulled away, still in one piece.

We once again rolled into the summit of the San Bernardino with its café, small lake and flagpole. The flag was still flicking playfully in the breeze. Shane was last to roll up. He jumped off the 750GS and circled the bike, reaching in and around the panniers and then scrutinising the hand guards and bodywork. I got the feeling that he'd had a little bit more of an experience than we'd had. I'd not seen what happened from up front and the incident was described to us by Dan, who had seen the drama play out in front of him. "Sideways and on fire," he concluded with a smirk. It was a stark reminder that the hairpins (and traffic) we were now so accustomed to could still bite back.

Luckily there was no real visible damage, other than a slight and hardly noticeable scuff, and so, stopping for little more than a comfort break, we used their facilities and pressed on down the opposite side of the pass.

We were making good time and had soon cleared Mesocco. I had been watching the clock, as I had an alternative route up my sleeve. A slight sightseeing detour, if you will.

Many months earlier it had come up in conversation that the dam facility that features in James Bond 007's *Goldeneye* was in Switzerland. I had checked its location on the map to find it was only thirty minutes off our route. The film sees James bungee jump off the Verzasca Dam, and with no further marketing encouragement needed, they had now set themselves up as a bungee-jumping tourist attraction. They claim to be the most famous bungee jump in the world, but with the jump being 220m, they are certainly one of the biggest.

When it was first discussed, the cost had put everyone off. I say everyone, I was never 'on' to be put off. I could probably say that for Nick, Brian and Eddie, whatever they might claim to the contrary. It was therefore left out of the final route and itinerary, but I had kept a separate printout of the route and a waypoint on the GPS that would allow me to deviate from the route we were on.

I didn't say anything to anyone, and I suspect that they were none the wiser as I peeled off the route just beyond Lumino. The more astute of them may have suspected that I was up to something since the route to the dam took us through an industrial zone and a heavily built up area. This is something that I would usually avoid and would pick a more refined route around. If they did suspect, then they didn't say anything.

Any suspicion would have evaporated in the heat as we started the short climb and the massive structure came into view. To say that the Verzasca Dam is huge is an understatement and its massive grey facia loomed ever larger as we drew closer and then parked up the bikes some fifty yards from the dam. The scale evident from the people stood on the dam that looked like ants from our current location.

At the centre we could see the rigging that formed the bungee jump and the bungees themselves dangled far below like a jungle vine. We wondered how any jumper would not make contact with the steep wall but as we walked closer you could see that the concave structure allowed anyone brave enough to jump with ample clearance to bounce and swing before being hoisted back up to the observing crowds peering over the handrail.

We proceeded to walk across the dam and to the centre. Peering over the edge to the floor far below to where Bond would have shot his grappling gun to reach the bottom rather than bounce around on the elastic cord like our participants were about to do.

Looking at the schedule, we had a batch of jumpers about to gear up and we also discovered that they were booked up. This was a relief, as they had joked that they were going to club together and pay for me to jump as a 'thank you' for putting the trip together.

The first jumper walked out. Adorned with harnesses and GoPro cameras, they attached his ankles to the bungee cord that had just been hoisted up. With a final briefing, they shuffled him up to the jump's edge on the overhanging scaffolding. After a brief pause, he jumped, immediately questioning his life choices. I suspect he wanted to shout something cool, but despite his mouth being open, his lungs had frozen and he was silent in fear as he plummeted to the rocks below.

He reached the extent of his drop and the stretched bungee cord yanked him back skyward. A second later his voice returned, and he was able to produce a celebratory yell, relived to complete the jump and not die. The winch descended and he was dragged back up to the platform.

The process was repeated for two further jumpers and we watched on before taking in the view down the valley leading off into the distance to Lake Maggiore before heading back from the dam. I don't need to jump off a dam for my thrills, I have an adventure bike.

On the way up to the dam, I'd pre-selected a couple of candidates for lunch, knowing that we would be retracing our steps to get back on our original route. It was by no means the hottest day we had experienced at thirty-six degrees, but the sun was strong, and it was a dry and overbearing heat, so pulling onto a dusty and baked lay-by, I was desperate for the shade of the restaurant opposite.

To the rear of a beige, featureless building, whose only indication of purpose was an old sign stating 'Ristorante', was an outdoor seating area shaded by half a dozen parasols. Further shade being provided by a large sycamore with its broad, maple-like leaves. The tree's sizeable trunk emanating from the courtyard and its peeling bark giving the impression of a camouflage pattern. The place was empty, but one other customer sat finishing a drink, and under the shade of the parasols and sycamore, we removed as much of our gear as was decent to do.

We arranged the tables so we could accommodate everyone, and sat down, waiting for service. The table was initially empty other than a fly swatter, which had been picked up by Shane. The flies were numerous in this outdoor area, appearing as if to annoy you on purpose, disappearing before you could react only to return some seconds later.

Shane sat inspecting his newfound weapon. He flexed its handle and took a couple of test swipes to assess its weight like a music conductor of extermination. Then, when he was suitably happy, he brought it down on the table. A fly lay motionless and with another flick it was discarded to the floor. Again, he brought down the swatter, and another fly was cast away. He continued his symphony of insect slaughter, keeping count of his tally, as the waitress approached.

We ordered our much-needed drinks and worked our way through another menu written in a foreign tongue. Everyone was getting much better at reading the menus, and a pattern of spotting and ordering regular favourites was emerging. As the drinks arrived at the table, Shane tossed down his weapon of fly destruction and announced, "Eighteen," as he awaited the next challenger.

Nick picked up the swatter and took out a couple more of the irritating pests. As he scanned for the next victim, Eddie reached for the swatter, prematurely wanting a turn. "Get off!" warned Nick as they squabbled over the plastic utensil. Meanwhile, Greg had been looking over the menu studiously and had enquired to the waitress what *cavallo* was. The waitress informed him that it was Italian for horse and unperturbed, he thought he might as well and put in his order.

Our food arrived, with Greg's steak arriving on a hot stone, uncooked. As he sliced off a small chunk, he offered some to Shane and Dan to try. It was still cold and raw, but although taken off guard at the discovery, he continued to chew away at the meat with a slightly perplexed expression, wondering if this was how it was supposed to be eaten. Greg was continuing to slice at the steak, pressing each piece onto the stone in an attempt to cook the meat on its diminishing heat. I looked on with amusement while eating my caprese salad.

Back at the bikes and again in the heat of the afternoon sun, I left it until the last second to put my jacket back on and after fastening my helmet's strap, struggled to get my gloves onto my sweating palms. With not even the slightest breeze, the sooner we could get moving and I could feel airflow though the vents of the jacket the better.

Picking up the original route at Gorduno, it was a largely uneventful run through the valley that follows the river Ticino, the route punctuated by the occasional tunnel. There was the option of leaving the E35 for the more roads that it was bypassing that lay parallel to it, but we had an eye on the time.

Looking at the ETA on the satnav, I realised that we had spent longer on the Verzasca Dam watching jumpers and murdering flies at lunch than expected. The original route would have taken us to Hospental where we could pick up the Furka. We would then loop around on the Nufenen (which we now knew was the pass Nick had been recalling with his references to the Fusion) to our overnight stop in Bedretto. With the Furka already ridden, I didn't think it at the detriment of the trip to skip this and have a taster of the Tremola before heading up the Nufenen and backtracking to our hotel.

At Chiggiogna, I saw an opportunity to pull off the main route to make the adjustments. Riding into a large parking area, a rider and his pillion were stood next to a GS in the otherwise-empty lot. I stuck my bike in what little shade was available and prodded the screen of the GPS while the others strolled over to the other travellers.

The couple were from Denmark, but the guy spoke perfect English; so much so that I initially thought he was American, but he was military and had spent time at Ft Bragg in the US. His pillion girlfriend listened on but didn't speak. I suspect her silence was because she didn't speak fluently, not that she didn't have anything to say. She appeared to understand, however, as she listened to the conversation.

The GS was owned by his girlfriend's father and it had been borrowed for their trip. He had been having clutch issues and was happy to see a group with a couple of GSs ride into the lot. The catch point of the clutch was too close to the bar and he would catch his fingers before the clutch plates released.

The suspicion was he had some air in his hydraulic clutch. Greg assisted and rolled out the adjustment as a quick fix. That seemed to do the trick and they continued to talk about where they had come from and where they were going. Our group reciprocated with tales of the Stelvio, which remained something of an in-joke, as any mention of it usually followed with the question, "Are we doing it today?"

With their clutch issues seemingly solved, the riders suited up and left. I had finished my adjustments and signalled to everyone that I was ready to depart. Once again, with the next waypoint of Airolo dialled in, we got back on the motorway and into yet another tunnel.

I spotted the exit for Airolo as it was simultaneously announced on my headset. I flicked on the indicator and quickly glanced in my mirror to confirm that the group had done the same. Happy that everyone had formed an orderly queue behind me, I peeled off onto the exit ramp and into the town.

Airolo marks the start of the Gotthard Pass highway (National Road 2), which was opened in 1977, and the road tunnel motorway, which opened in 1980. The latter was, at the time, the world's longest road tunnel until 2000. And while there has been a bridle path since the thirteenth century, we were heading for the old paved pass dating back from 1830. With a maximum height of 2,106m, the Tremola San Gottardo climbs 300m in twenty-four hairpin bends of cobbled road.

Turning off the main road that passes through Airolo onto a side street, the GPS indicated that this would lead to the start of the Tremola. As we rounded the next corner, our path was blocked by cones and barriers, and behind numerous workmen digging up the road. The bikes concertinaed together, and I signalled I was going to find another way around, if indeed that was possible. The Tremola had been one of the highlights of my previous trip and to miss it would be infuriating.

I was zooming out on the GPS screen and trying to manually find a way around as we traversed the tight residential roads at the back of the town. Thinking I'd spotted the way, we rounded the residences and came around for another go, only to arrive at the exact same spot where we had started. The workmen looked on at the same group of bikes returning with curiosity. There must be a way around, surely, they just can't shut the whole road without a diversion. Could they? Not wanting another abortive loop, I thought that it would be best to take a closer look at the map.

As I had suspected, there was another access road when approached from the lower road through the town. I picked up the main road through Airolo, passing the central rail terminal and out though the other side before picking up the right-hand turn. We emerged on the opposite side of the roadworks and with a clear route ahead of us, we rode away from the road workers.

The road we were on leads to both the Tremola and the newer Gotthard Pass, and after a couple of attempts we found the sign indicating the correct route to the Tremola. After some initial doubts that it actually was the correct road, the paved surface switched to cobbles and the Tremola San Gottardo opened up before us.

After so many miles of smooth roads, the cobbled surface felt peculiar as the tyres skipped occasionally on the hairpin bends, but while the sensation was unusual, the bikes were ultimately sure-footed. Confident that we had a dry surface, we attacked the climb with an increasing pace. If wet, I fear the surface would have been extremely treacherous.

As the open tunnel of the newer Gotthard Pass came into view, I stopped the bikes so that we could dismount and get a view of the road we had climbed, albeit only halfway. The scene offers an impressive contrast, with the newer engineering of the pass looming overhead and the older, but no less obsolete, road climbing up to where they two roads intersect.

We turned the bikes around and headed back down towards Airolo. We would return tomorrow to ride the full length of the Tremola, but for now, this was just a taste and, seeing that we were on a revised route, I wanted to make sure that we could make it up to the summit of the Nufenen before the day drew to a close.

The road from Airolo to the Nufenen runs straight off the Gotthard Pass, so we avoided any the unnecessary trips around the town that we had encountered previously. After the tight cobbled turns of the Tremola, it was nice for us all to stretch the legs of the bikes, the big twin of the 1200GS thumping into life and behind me a symphony of noise with the pair of growling 750GSs, the snarling XR, the whistling triple of the Triumph and the howling K1300S.

The road was long and relatively straight, and we continued

at a good pace until the road started to climb up to the pass, with switchbacks appearing with increasing frequency. As the hairpins straightened, the throttles could be opened again. We were enjoying the ascent and riding in the zone, as coming towards us a rider waved his arm, signalling that we should slow down.

With our previous encounter with the Polizia still fresh in my mind, I grabbed a fist-full of brake and scrubbed off a chunk of speed. Behind me, Dan had been in a different zone and had been watching the mountain goats we had been passing with their impressive horns. He turned his gaze away from the goats and back towards the back of my bike which he was gaining on at an alarming rate.

I glanced in my mirrors to see if the rest of the group had noted the signal to see the whites of Dan's eyes, with his front wheel only inches from mine. As his brake pads bit into the front disk, he dropped away, heart pumping just that little bit faster than it had seconds earlier.

I rounded the next few bends, expecting to see either the police or some other obstruction, but there was nothing, and I was left wondering what he had been trying to tell us as I led us onto the loose gravel of the apron at the top of the pass.

The Nufenen Pass is the highest paved pass in Switzerland at 2,478m, and links Airolo to Brig. From the vantage point at the top of the Nufenen, you could be forgiven for thinking that you are at the top of the world. A vast expanse of mountain peaks stretched out as far as the eye could see, some shrouded in clouds, others bold against the blue sky. Residual snow laced the peaks and a wall of white still remained either side of us between the gift shop and café at opposite ends of the parking area.

After throwing a few well-meant taunts at Nick and his newly imagined Fusion Pass, Dan and Shane climb over the snowbanks to get a better view of the Nufenen landscape below, while Eddie headed for the souvenir shop. Returning from their short trek, Dan and Shane joined Nick and Brian, who had spotted a Maclaren which had rolled up, and they were heading for a closer look. The air was tranquil and calm, and I stood enjoying the stunning view. The stillness was only broken when the wasp-like buzz of Greg's drone saw it shoot into the air high above. He had spotted a track coming down the pass just off the road and wanted a closer look.

The drone had made a couple of earlier appearances, notably over the pastures and single track near the Jaun Pass and over the waters of Lake Thun. Their diminishing size and price have seen them gain popularity over the last few years. The DJI that Greg had folded into a case not much bigger than an overnight toiletries bag and very easy to carry on the bike.

I must admit I am tempted, but I sometimes find my ground-based, bike-attached GoPro cameras a chore to feed with memory cards and batteries while travelling. I have over the years made a conscious effort to reduce my dependence on things that need charging, having to transport and store the chargers required. I'd got my dependence down to two GoPro cameras, with one on the bike and one on my helmet. I no longer carried a camera and for many years had used nothing else but my phone.

The drone came back around; at first you could only hear its buzz, but then, from a speck in the distance, it came into sight, flying at speed over where we stood. I positioned myself behind Greg so I could see the screen over his shoulder. While the footage recorded can make a spectacular YouTube video, Greg was using the drone to scan the landscape for interesting features and alternative routes from the high (very high) vantage point.

The drone was now hundreds of feet above our location.

Having seen enough through the eyes of the drone, Greg brought the device gently to the ground. Folding in its blades and replacing the protective covers, it was popped back in its case, zipped up and put back in the top case of his bike. The controller was stored in a second case and the screen returned to its original function as a smartphone.

It was time to head back down and get checked in at the hotel. It wasn't too late, but I'd booked us into a swanky-looking hotel and spa in Bedretto, and wanted to make sure we made the best of it rather than just hitting the sack.

I rolled the bike around and headed back to the road. Turning left out of the car park before opening the throttle and pulling away at a similar pace to which we had arrived. Nick was puzzled, since the hotel and the direction we had come from was opposite to where I was going. I heard him say something to that effect in the communicator headset but couldn't make out exactly what he had said. There were no further protests and, without asking for clarification of what the original message was, I carried on.

It was much further down the far side of the Nufenen that I started to realise I wasn't recognising the scenery from our earlier ascent and pulled up. Now devoid of any wind noise, Nick repeated what he had tried to inform me of earlier. "It was *right* out of the car park," he stated, leaving out the words, "you tit!" Since this conversation was being played out inside of our helmets only, I decided the best explanation to the rest of the group was that it was intentional, and I wanted them to experience the full Nufenen run. The group, however, was down by two.

As far as I was aware, there was only one road down to where we had stopped. I wondered if they had realised that I had taken off in the wrong direction and had headed directly for the hotel. The other possibility is that they had crashed, but given that we could see the road climbing back up the pass and that there was no evident wreckage hurtling down the mountainside, I went for best-case scenario. I hammered it back up the pass, with the remainder of the group following.

As we reached the summit and carried down the opposite side, the pack was starting to thin out as I kept up my brisk pace, anxious to find out where Greg and Shane were. As I approached the indicated turn-off at Bedretto, the pack had stretched a good mile and I pulled up to the hotel alone, the next two riders of Dan and Eddie arriving a short while later, followed by Nick and Brian. There was still no sign of Shane or Greg. It was obvious that the notion that they had headed for the hotel was incorrect.

I made my way into the hotel, a beautifully presented stone-clad building that was dripping with Alpine charm. It was framed against the mountains that were illuminated by the early evening sun. Balconies adorned with red and white flowers jutted out over a raised patio area. I entered from the lower floor with the aforementioned patio, the bar and restaurant on the first floor.

The décor had a ski-resort charisma, with sheepskins draped over leather sofas and antique skis ornamenting the walls. I entered the bar area, feeling a little out of place in the plush surroundings dressed in my now-grubby adventure suit, visibly soiled from a number of days on the road. I was greeted, however, with a smile and once I had introduced myself, was handed the keys to two suites. The rooms I had booked accommodated ten people in total and we had ample space to relax in style.

I returned to the bikes, which were being unloaded, and handed a key to one of the suites to Dan before continuing with the usual ritual of stripping the bike of luggage. Tossing the roll sack over my shoulder, I picked up my remaining pannier bag and, impatient to enjoy the facilities, left the bike unlocked and headed back to the room. The location was so tranquil and remote, I couldn't imagine any possible criminality occurring.

Nick was first through the door, quickly bagging the double bed on the ground floor of the suite. The remaining beds were in an upper floor area accessed from the lounge by an open wooden staircase, so steep it was on the borderline of being called a ladder. The opposite suite was similar, minus the lounge area, with an upper area with single beds. The double in this suite had been selected by Eddie, who was already, at this stage, heading for the shower as the remaining guests selected their beds, with the exception of Shane and Greg, who were still missing.

There was no concern at this stage as we mulled over the possibilities and concluded that they had just gone off for a blast. And this is exactly what had happened. When using the drone earlier, Greg has spotted that the small track leading away from the road led into a valley up to where its path was blocked by a huge bank of snow that was yet to fully thaw. Another road led to a dammed lake.

The 750GS was an accomplished adventure bike and although on road tyres, Greg had suggested to Shane that they should get the full experience by exploring these roads and the surrounding landscape.

Peeling off from the pack, they had hopped off the road and onto the smaller track. The track ran up towards the Ägene river and after a number of hairpins, tailed off to a rocky track, whose path was ultimately blocked by the large bank of snow that they had viewed from the Nufenen summit, its melted water feeding the river. The surface beneath the tyres was mainly gravel and wet from the water that was running off the mountain, and crossing a stream, they then blasted up the hill with some momentum to keep the tyres working. A wildlife ranger's truck sat in front of the snowdrift, but the ranger was nowhere to be seen. With no possibility of going further, they returned back towards the road.

The second track led up to the Griessee, a small lake fed from the Gries Glacier situated in the Lepontine Alps. At one edge of the Griessee, a hydroelectric dam had been constructed, and this had contributed to the increased retreat of the glacier as the water levels had decoupled the ice from the bedrock beneath. Picking up the track from the Nufenen Pass, they travelled a short way but again found their path blocked by snow. After a brief attempt to ride over it, they found it to be too soft and thinking better of it, headed back to meet us at the hotel.

Back at the hotel, we had soon all washed and changed, and met in the bar where a table had been set. We reviewed the day's activities while we waited for our meal. With Greg and Shane still discussing their off-road activity, I contemplated our adventure-riding credentials. Sat in such luxury surroundings, it was a far cry from the overland journeys that I had often followed in magazines, but despite not wild camping in the wilderness, I still felt that sense of adventure. We were living day to day with only what could be carried on a bike and we were riding some of the greatest motorcycling roads of the world.

The sun disappeared behind the mountains and darkness fell. It was a clear night and the air still retained some of the day's warmth. As we retired for bed and I climbed the wooden stairs to the lofted sleeping area like one of the von Trapp children in *The Sound of Music*, Greg was reaching for his riding gear once again. He took the GS back to the summit of the Nufenen and sat in the darkness and the cooler midnight air, the occasional shooting star darting across the sky in a scene of serenity.

Chapter Nine

Cowbells and Cheese

I AWOKE EARLY THE NEXT MORNING, MY PHONE indicating it was just past 5am, and I came down to find Shane crashed out on the sofa, having never made it to his bed. He lay motionless and just managed to open an eye in the morning light as I made a coffee with the supplies I found in the small kitchenette.

Taking my brew in hand, I walked out onto the small wooden balcony. I placed my coffee on the handrail and sat watching the steam rise from the mug. The sun was starting to rise, and its orange glow emanated from the mountains in front of me. The only sound in this idyllic setting was the rush of water from the shallow stream that ran alongside the road below. As the sun broke cover, its rays steamed over the peaks and I breathed the pure air deeply as I basked in its warmth.

One by one, everyone else made an appearance and I gathered up my gear ready to haul everything back down to the bike. With everything loaded, we headed back to the hotel bar and onto the patio area for breakfast in the bright sunshine.

The morning's route would first take us back to the Tremola that we had sampled the day before. We picked up the road to Airolo and started the short journey to the base of the pass. Taking the opportunity to refuel in Airolo, we then took the now-familiar turn onto the sequence of curves and junctions that split the Tremola from the newer Gotthard Pass. Approaching the sprawling junction, we once again missed the turn and found ourselves on the Gotthard.

Accepting the mistake, and now committed to the road, I justified the error by reminding myself that I had never been on this stretch before. I could just tick it off the list and on the other side pick up the Tremola from the top. As it turns out, it was a mistake that worked in our favour. High up in the open tunnelled section, we approached roadworks and a red light. This was the section that we had viewed from the Tremola way below. From this vantage point and having the time to take in the scene, having been halted by the traffic light, we could see the whole Tremola in all its glory laid out before us. The road's many curves cascaded down the side of the mountain like a cobbled ribbon.

The light flicked to green and we continued to meet our objective at the small group of lakes that sit 2,106m at the top of the Gotthard Pass.

Picking up the Tremola from the top is much easier than from below. There are none of the sprawling road layouts that had caused so much previous confusion. We peeled off the smooth paved surface onto the cobbles and started the descent. Hairpin after hairpin, we negotiated the tight curves with each bike's suspension working overtime, as we rode down the road that we had earlier observed form our lofty viewpoint. Soon we levelled off and reached the bottom.

Turning around to indicate that this was where we would be turning around to pick up on the initial route, I saw that Greg and Shane had once again improvised an off-road excursion and were bouncing over rocks and boulders on the far side of a stream. We watched on with amusement as the two adventurers negotiated the terrain, emerging back onto the road, broad grins on their faces within their helmets.

Dan was once again on the XR and he led the charge back up the Tremola, the rest of us chasing behind, once again emerging onto the Gotthard. After a brief stop to allow Eddie to get his souvenir sticker, we continued on towards Hospental and then on to Andermatt.

As we approached Andermatt, we turned onto the road that would give us both the opportunity to grab a drink and also ride through the centre of the village. Having grabbed a drink at the Hotel Aurora (famous for being where James Bond fills up his Aston Martin after his Furka car chase), we continued past the improvised statue of a mounted Kawasaki GPz550 with a bear astride its seat and onto the narrow cobbled street.

Andermatt is a pretty and typically Swiss village located at the centre of the Saint-Gotthard Massif. Although we were passing through, it provides an excellent base for motorcyclists, being central to many of the well-known passes. Wooden buildings line each side of the road, with numerous flags of Switzerland and the region decorating the facias. We emerged on the other side of the village, passing the fuel station where we had filled up some days earlier and departed.

We approached Wassen, picking up the sign for the Susten Pass, and started a steady climb, with only the occasional gentle curve. The road soon threw a couple of hairpin bends at us and we pulled off the road at an observation deck not far from its 2,260m summit. The Susten Pass would take us through to Innertkirchen, from where I had planned a change of scenery with a route through Emmental farming pastures.

We re-joined the road and soon rode over the summit and the climb became a descent. The traffic on the Susten was a little heavier than previous roads, but that was of no concern, and we cruised past the cars with ease. I was keeping a good pace up front and Eddie had tucked in behind me, having informed me that if I felt he was a little close, it was because he was getting some video footage. And so, in this formation, we were overtaking in tight formation and passed a few more cars and the occasional bike.

Approaching a set of temporary lights, a longer queue of vehicles had come to a halt. We tucked in behind them as a procession of cars came the opposite direction, released with a green light. As they filed past and our light turned green, a Supermoto that I had earlier overtaken shot past my left-hand side. Nick's voice came over the communicator: "He's been pissed off ever since you passed him." Amused by this, I pulled into the opposite lane and accelerated past the stationary cars, and then overtook the couple of cars ahead that had already pulled away from the traffic lights.

I was soon on the tail of the other bike who, glancing in his mirror, realised I was behind him and noticeably adjusted his posture as he tried to race away. I would point out that at no point was this a race, but I was entertained by the notion that I had annoyed him with my earlier overtake with a fully laden GS. I certainly wasn't going to allow him the satisfaction of pulling away from me. I was going to stay in his mirrors all the way down the pass.

I cranked open the throttle through the next couple of curves and positioned myself to take the approaching left-hand bend. As I tipped the bike in, a coach rounded the corner, taking more of the road that it should have crossing the central line. I grabbed the brake and sat the bike up as the front of the bus whistled past my helmet. Expletives emanated from my helmet as I once again threw the bike into an ever-diminishing bend once clear of the unwanted hazard.

Accident avoided and my head still attached, my tormented

friend had gained 100 yards on me. Cracking open the throttle once again, I used every available part of rubber as I flung it through the last few bends, catching the foot pegs on the road surface as the suspension compressed through the apex. I was soon in his mirrors once again. We were coming off the pass and approaching a small village, and as I saw him glance at me in his mirror, I decided that my little game of cat and mouse was over, stopping to wait for the others.

Our final destination for the day was Grindelwald. To head there directly would have seen us there in time for lunch and half a riding day wasted. When I was planning the route and browsing the maps, I used the good old rule of thumb: look for somewhere green. This was always a good indication that you were away from built-up areas and could almost be guaranteed some good roads.

In this case, I looked to the area north of Lake Brienz, where the map had shown the large green area labelled 'UNESCO Biosphäre Entlebuch'. At the foot of the Alps, in the Swiss Canton of Lucerne, the Entlebuch Biosphere is a natural reserve that in September 2001 became the second UNESCO Biosphere Reserve in Switzerland, after the Swiss National Park.

It's an area of pastures, unspoilt moorlands and craggy karst rock formations. Close to the Emmental region, where the famous cheese of the same name is made, the pastures are filled with grazing cows and the sound of their bells permeates through the air. It would serve as a contrasting illustration of Switzerland form the high mountain passes.

I had attempted to ride the area some years prior with Nick and Brian. On that occasion we rode through some of the worst rain I have ever encountered and as we climbed higher into the region, we actually rode into the low clouds that had descended, which rendered our visibility to literally a few metres. We had been caught out and could find no shelter to put on our wet weather gear and by the time we did, it was too late, and the rain had already seeped through the shower-proof material of our suits. We aborted our planned ride and took the fast route out towards Bern, hoping to get dry at our overnight stop in Lauterbrunnen.

Today, however, the weather was once again dry with only a hint of cloud in the sky. Stopping briefly for lunch in Brünig, we continued past the waters of Lungernsee, turning onto the twisting Glaubenbielen Pass at Giswil. The road climbed through a hilly expanse of farmland, punctuated by agricultural buildings and then into woodland. Breaking out of the woodland, a panorama of valleys stretched out below, covered by a blanket of fir trees.

Behind us a field of cows grazed and as Dan, Shane, Greg and Eddie approached, they looked up curiously and one by one approached the adventure-suited visitors. As more of the herd followed suit, the gentle sound of the occasional bell rose to a crescendo of noise, with dozens of cows on the move. The bell hung from thick leather collars around their neck.

In these Alpine regions, when the snow has melted in the spring, villages send the cows to the high Alpine meadows to graze in an event called *Alpaufzug*. The event is celebrated with a procession through the village to the high pastures, with floral wreaths decorating the cow's horns. The best milk-producing cow in the village leads the procession and wears the largest bell.

Of the cows in front of us, some wore a simple copper 'Trychel' bell of various sizes, others carrying large cast brass bells, indicating their milk-producing prowess. Shane had, at this point, decided that they needed further reward for services to milk production. Equipped with one of our tour stickers that had been used at every opportunity to tag every available surface, he jumped the fence and was in the field.

We watched on in amusement as he strolled between the cows, trying not to startle them with his presence. He approached one of the cows, who was still eating the grass. It paused and then raised its head as he lay his hand on its shoulder, but as he reached around to apply the sticker to the bell, it pulled away and trotted off.

After a couple more abortive attempts, he found himself walking at a steady pace alongside another target. I glanced over his shoulder to another of the beasts that seemed quite alert and was watching and wondering what all the fuss was. Unlike the other cows, this had horns. I briefly entertained the idea that this was a bull and we would be entertained by a diminutive Shane flying out of the field in rodeo style at the behest of the bull's horns. Lowering my gaze, however, I spotted a dangling set of udders.

Seizing the opportunity, Shane delivered the sticker to the bell of the cow he had been walking alongside. He turned with a look of accomplishment, a broad grin across his face as he chuckled to himself. The cow strolled off, oblivious. As we returned to the bikes, we wondered what puzzled reaction the farmer would have on finding the new decoration.

We rode on into the Entlebuch Biosphere and through Flühli. Differing from previous days riding at altitude and over mountains, we were now riding a much flatter route through the valley surrounded by green pastures with flecks of colour from the wildflowers. Any changes in gradient were gradual and the run was at a much more relaxed pace. Perhaps overly so. As we dropped onto main road near Schüpfheim, I was feeling uninspired by the flat landscape.

At Entlebuch, we turned onto the Glaubenberg Pass; the scenery improved and the road became more engaging.

Maybe a little too much so for an unknown rider coming the opposite direction. Nick was on the left side of his lane on a blind corner. The oncoming bike appeared in his lane, his luggage extending either side. Both riders jerked their bikes hard right, and then within a fraction of a second Nick swung his bike back left, narrowly avoiding a clash of panniers, with less than an inch between them. All of this was observed by Eddie riding behind, who was convinced that if Nick had not taken such instinctive action, then they would have collided.

The riders up front were blissfully unaware of the drama that had unfolded behind them and, approaching the run down to Lake Sarnen, broke through the cover of the trees. A huge expanse of snow-capped mountains stretched for as far as the eye could see. The subtle incline had not given us a feel that we were climbing, but from this vantage point we could see the scale of the surrounding landscape.

We stopped at a roadside hotel for a stretch of the legs and some refreshments. The sky had clouded and while it wasn't raining, the air was much cooler. By the time we had drunk coffee we could see the odd speck of rain. While others dug out the rain gear, I opted just to zip up the air vents on my jacket and trousers.

The threat of rain had fizzled out and had proven to be just a brief shower. I was happy that we had completed the run in decent weather, although perhaps if I had been able to see more of the run on my last trip I might have been persuaded to pick an alternative route, perhaps a couple of loops of the Susten, Grimsel and Furka.

Riding on the south shore of Lake Brienz, we turned off the highway at Interlaken, not to go directly to Grindelwald but first to visit Lauterbrunnen. Earning the title of the Swiss Yosemite because of its steep vertical rockfaces and cascading waterfalls, Lauterbrunnen lies on the opposite side of the Eiger from Grindelwald and at the base of the Jungfrau.

We followed the road into Lauterbrunnen; the rockface rose steeply either side of the road. On the right, a stream of water spectacularly began its descent from many metres high above. On the left a green hill carrying a railway line up its steep side before being interrupted by the tall rockface of the mountains that dominated the skyline. In front of us a narrow valley cut its way into the distance between the immense rock formations.

We followed the street through the town, with its Alpine buildings dwarfed by the scale of the surroundings and funnelled into a car park at the base of the 300m-high Staubbach Falls. While we stood looking at the impressive waterfall, its dramatic drop down a stark rockface of beige and grey stone from an upper fringe of trees, Dan went to take a closer look. A zig-zag staircase of steps led up to a viewing platform where the water crashed into the rocks below. This was far too much effort for the rest of us, and we milled around the bikes waiting for him to return.

Over the past couple of days, it was becoming apparent that Eddie was constantly working his way up the pack. This may have been a direct result of the speeding tickets we had been issued back in Campascio, where it was the front and last rider that got the ticket. We were sat on the bikes while we waited for Dan to return from his hike.

Brian sat to my left and to his left sat Eddie. Nick was over on the opposite side of the car park with Shane and Gregg, and they had been discussing a plan as my communicator crackled into life and Nick explained their nefarious plan.

Knowing that Eddie didn't want to ride at the back, they would circle the car park and make a bolt for the exit when they could be sure that the order of bikes left the Triumph playing rearguard. It was all in good spirits, and Eddie was unaware of the plotting as the only people paired with my communicator were Brian and Nick. I contributed to the plan, realising that there was a second exit where I would be able to jump to the front while everyone else left via the main outlet.

The plan was executed without fault and we rode out of Lauterbrunnen, with my GS leading, in a tight formation to prevent any queue jumping. We have no idea if Eddie even knew of the plot and at the time of writing I still don't. He will, of course, read this.

There is only one way in and out of Lauterbrunnen; the same can be said about Grindelwald. By vehicle, anyway, the road to both locations from Interlaken sits like an inverted 'Y', and we soon reached the fork in the road, peeling off right to head to Grindelwald.

The open road soon reduced to a tree-covered valley, which tightened until giving way to a mountainous view. The Eiger to the right, with the Jungfrau peeking over its shoulder and the Mettenberg up ahead. It had once been suggested to me when Lauterbrunnen was brought up in a conversation that I should try Grindelwald as an alternative, and I could see why as we rolled into the village. It was typically Swiss and surrounded by stunning mountains. The village was bustling with tourists, but what were we but tourists ourselves? We had travelled and stayed in quieter areas, but now, as we approached the final stages of the tour, we were happy for some more lively nightlife.

We rolled up to the hotel and before we could dismount were greeted by the hotel staff, who ushered us into the hotel's sheltered parking bays before returning with the keys to our room. A lift took us to the upper floor where we dumped our bags and, emerging onto the balcony, found an unhindered view of the Eiger before us and the village of Grindelwald below.

Trees lined the base of the mountains before the rockface rose to the sky, laced with clouds around their peaks. The familiar noise of the electric trains could be heard in the air as they worked their way down the hillside on their journey from Lauterbrunnen on the opposite side.

I retreated back into the room and went through the usual ritual of swapping memory cards in the cameras and placing the batteries on charge, then took the opportunity to freshen up my pannier bag with some fresh clothes. We were on the final stages of the trip and the vacuum bag of clean clothes in the roll bag was getting smaller as the second bag of dirty clothes was getting bigger.

One day, I told myself, I'd wash these clothes on a journey rather than take them home. One day I might travel around the world with a tent and a sleeping bag. But for now, I sat on my comfy hotel bed waiting for my turn to shower, flicking through my TripAdvisor app looking for a swanky restaurant.

We strolled down to Barry's, a Swiss restaurant within one of the hotels in the heart of the town. We'd spotted it on the app and it had good reviews. I wondered if the Barry referred to the famous St Bernard breed of dog. The name 'St Bernard' originates from the Great St Bernard Hospice, the traveller's hospice on the Great St Bernard Pass we had travelled over some days before. The dogs were called 'Alpenmastiff', or 'Barry Dogs', before the name St Bernard became more widespread.

Grindelwald seemed a hive of activity, with tourists strolling through the shops and past the restaurants. It was a fine evening and through the air could be heard the soundtrack of an impromptu outdoor cinema of a film festival that was ongoing. We soon found Barry's through the entrance of one of the hotels in the centre.

The wooden-lined walls and dimmed lighting gave the place a particular atmosphere that juxtaposed with the glass-panelled modern lines of a smoking room, with its walls lined with fine wines and a humidor of cigars in the corner.

Over the evening meal, we discussed the options for our final day of travel. It would be a short day on the road. Not only would we have to get back to Thoiry and get the UK-bound bikes checked back onto the Bikeshuttle, but the rental bikes would need returning. I had planned a route, which tried to pick us some good roads, but with some outstanding riding already under our belts, we opted to take a simpler journey back through to Geneva.

Chapter Ten

Back to Geneva and Journey's End

THE FOLLOWING MORNING CAME, AND WE RETRACED our steps, leaving Grindelwald behind us on the way back to Interlaken. I recalled seeing a garage with a number of jet wash bays on our inbound run. Knowing that the rentals had a few scuff and bangs, we thought that it would be less noticeable if we at least removed the road grime of the last week. As we pulled into the bays, lining the bikes up so we could wash as many as possible on a single coin, it amused me that we were so far from a 'long way' adventure that we couldn't even let the bikes get dirty. Besides, I was convinced that our sleight-of-hand tactic of 'Never mind the broken bits; look at them shine!' was foolproof.

The troop of somewhat-cleaner motorcycles rolled out, reached Interlaken and settled in formation to cruise the longer but faster route via Bern to Lausanne, then on to Geneva.

I'm not an enthusiast of motorway miles by any stretch of the imagination, but over the years I've become more used to them. This is largely down to the big GS. Its comfort and ability to eat the miles is a long way from the runs I used to do on the S1000RR Superbike. I often don't settle on a long run until my mind wanders off to those long stints up and around Scotland. I could just about manage an hour before my legs seized and I'd have to stop. But now two, even three hours could pass, and I'd be quite happy.

I glanced in my mirrors, expecting to see a staggered formation of bikes taking my lead as I pulled into the inside lane to pass a slower car and then pull back in when clear. What I saw was a pair of 750GSs and a 1200GS performing a pincer movement on a Tiger 800.

A chuckling voice came over the radio from the S1000XR behind them. Instead of settling in for the duration of the ride, they had decided that they were going to continue the game of 'Eddie at the Rear' and were co-ordinating their formation over their communicators – Eddie unaware of the planned strategy, but at this stage I suspect he knew. I told a still-chortling Nick I'd give them space and waited for Eddie, now free of his captives, to approach me. I opened up the GS, which lurched forward, its torque allowing it to pull away from the Triumph with ease. I looked back at the groups to see another pincer movement forming and Eddie being pushed back down the order.

The game continued for a number of miles, and soon, if not only because of this distraction but also by the additional pace the game had encouraged, we arrived at a service station and pulled off.

The services at Lully were notable not only for the mounted Swiss Air Force Dassault Mirage III sitting aloft of the car park on a concrete plinth, suspended in animation as if doing a fly-past, but also a sex shop. "Negative ghost rider, the pattern is full," I exclaimed.

Hang on, back up a bit… A sex shop, in a service station, amidst the coffee shops and McDonald's?!

We had stopped at Lully on a previous trip and were taken

aback to find the Magic X Erotic Megastore shop sat within the services, a neatly arranged display of rabbit vibrators, love eggs and butt plugs for all to see. I know that the Europeans are a little less prudish than the British, but in a service station?

Regardless of our initial reaction, I had told the American travellers of this as if it was going to be the highlight of the trip, and the pinnacle of the tour across the Alpine valleys and passes. I knew it would appeal to them and I knew they had yet to find a suitable souvenir to take home for their partners.

It was with immense disappointment that we entered the food court and peeled off towards the toilets to find the store had been replaced with a gift shop. Perhaps their DVD sales had declined, and they had gone the way of Blockbuster, or perhaps online shopping had dented their adult toy sales, or maybe, just maybe, someone had realised that a gift shop would be a little more appropriate in such an environment.

Those that needed a comfort break headed for the toilets, then headed into the gift shop, eyeing up the various caps, shirts, mugs, tea towels, bottle openers, fridge magnets, in fact anything possible that could be produced in red with the white Swiss cross on it.

I strolled off to get a McDonald's banana milkshake, and if the disappointment of the lack of erotic megastore wasn't enough, I was told they only had strawberry or vanilla. "Whatever, strawberry."

I skulked off with my shake and were soon joined by the others with their grown-up coffee beverages. I sucked at the thick milkshake while we reviewed the plan. We had cracked off half the route and were in good time for our rendezvous with the Bikeshuttle. The local bars would be open and I was looking forward to putting my feet up with a beer while the rental bikes were returned.

The Polizia were loitering on an access road as we returned

to the bikes, and I hoped we had not overstepped the limits with our earlier shenanigans. They seemed uninterested in us as we left, to my relief, and after a quick refuel, we went on our way.

We watched our backs on the final run into Geneva, the many overhead cameras eyeing our progress, particularly on the entrances to the frequent tunnels. My focus was on my GPS map as the road layouts became more complex on the arrival to Geneva, more so by the roadworks throwing up temporary lanes. With a final check of the mirrors to make sure I had everyone behind me, I exited the motorway near the airport and onto the streets of Geneva.

It's a long straight road out of Geneva from the airport. A road that had been travelled well, given the baggage problems that we'd encountered, and while that experience was becoming a distant memory, the route was still very familiar. The previously used Shell fuel station on the right, the Nirvana Indian restaurant with its welcoming elephants on the left and through the CERN complex full of scientists. We were soon crossing the French/Swiss border outpost and were back in France.

The familiar site of the Best Western hotel at Thoiry soon came into sight. We had travelled some distance since we rolled out of the entrance on that Friday morning, but it seemed like it was only the day before. The rentals peeled off to the front of the hotel and I followed Nick and Brian to the back.

The Bikeshuttle lorry was already parked up to the rear of the hotel, the drivers still in their hotel rooms catching up on sleep for the journey back to the UK. One other inbound traveller had arrived before us and he was busy unpacking his bike as we rolled up and lined up alongside.

They had already lined up the boxes that would carry our gear and, not wanting to make unnecessary trips in the heat, I stripped off in the car park and threw a pair of shorts on. With the riding gear and helmets stowed, I grabbed my overnight bag and travel documents from the panniers. Another couple of bikes rolled up as we walked back to the hotel. They would soon be on the lorry and it would be tomorrow afternoon before we were once again reunited in the UK.

The American travellers still had the task of returning their rentals, and were removing their luggage and personal effects as we re-joined them at the front of the hotel. I was in wind-down mode, while part of me was disheartened that this part of the trip had come to a conclusion, another part of me was looking forward to a relaxing afternoon without the responsibility of riding. That could only mean a boozy session in the bar and I was relieved that I didn't have to go through the process of returning a rental while the bike was scrutinised for damage. They soon left. "Good luck," I mouthed as I waved them off through the gate.

Nick and I took our places at the front of the Italian restaurant next door and were soon greeted by a waitress whom we informed that part of our party would be joining us later, but for now we would just like a drink. It was another hot day; the sun being kept at bay by the awning at the front of the restaurant. The place was busy, but we didn't have to wait long before our beers arrived.

While I sat enjoying my cold beverage while talking about the past few days, it gave me a chance to reflect on the trip. As I've said before, despite any aspirations that I may harbour, I am not an around-the-world adventurer, and while it is true I have travelled and ridden motorcycles in many countries, I am not the type of person who can sell up and ride into the sunset.

What I hope I have demonstrated is that adventure can be affordable and on your doorstep. There is no less value in travelling 100 miles from home in a day than there is travelling thousands of miles over many months. Adventure is as much about enjoying the road, the scenery, the people you meet and the people you take with you, and maybe less about the miles you cover. I've had some of my best days on the shorter runs, as long as I have my motorcycle and the freedom to explore.

And so, nearing the end of this particular journey, I can fondly look back on the awe-inspiring majesty of the Combe Laval, the rides through forests with the smell of pine in the air, the thrill of the mountain passes with relentless switchbacks, the breathtaking views of the snow-capped Alpine mountain ranges, and the tranquil turquoise lakes that often appear in the most unlikely places.

It's not just the places that make a trip special, but also the shared experiences. With a questionable mix of characters from the US and the UK, we formed a common bond based on our love of two-wheeled travel. My close friends from across the pond had joined my close friends from home and I had the pleasure of introducing them to my European playground. I had the gratification of experiencing the first-time wonder of the Alps through their eyes and emotions.

I see many posts on the internet from travellers making an annual motorcycle pilgrimage across Europe. You may be one of them and in reading this, you recognise your own experiences. If you are someone who has yet to adventure travel, maybe having seen or read about people crossing continents over many months, I encourage you to try the Alps. You can achieve so much with a small amount of cost, both in money and time. While this trip is not across the dusty trails of Africa, or the wilds of South America, or even through the exotic landscapes of Asia, I hope it provides some form of inspiration for travel, albeit on the refined roads of Europe.

I finished my drink and indicated to the waitress that we

were ready to order food. Dan, Eddie, Greg and Shane were still on the other side of Geneva and over the border at the French rental company. They would be the best part of an hour at least and my stomach was angrily growling at me, despite the liquid lunch. The waitress approached the table only to inform us that the kitchen was now closed before scurrying back inside, leaving me loudly expressing my dismay. Looking at the time on my phone, I realised that the restaurant on the other side of the hotel was probably still open. Thankfully it was, just. Brian had been called away to take a business conference call, so Nick and myself ordered and were served food as more Bikeshuttle customers rolled up to be told that this kitchen was also now closed. Bloody French and their strange ways.

A taxi pulled up outside the hotel and the Americans emerged from its interior. The return of the bikes had gone relatively smoothly, and the rental place was not overly concerned at the condition of the bikes. There were a few charges for the odd scratch – notably one for a scratch Dan had picked up on the valve cover of the 1200GS engine and, of course, Shane's broken lever.

Typically, Eddie had been complaining about a deposit charge despite the rentals staff's amiable attitude, much to the discomfiture of his fellow travellers. Keys handed back, charges paid, they just wanted to get the taxi called to get back to us at the hotel. I should give credit to the company, Moto-Plaisir, for their excellent service. If you are coming from further afield and do not have the ability to arrive in the Alps with your own bike, I would definitely look them up. From the feedback I got, I'd have no hesitation in recommending them.

Enquiring at the hotel reception, we were informed that just a mile up the road was the small commune of Saint-Genis-Pouilly. Furthermore, they would be happy to drop us and some other Bikeshuttle customers off in their shuttle bus.

We piled into the bus and were, in a matter of minutes, climbing back out and heading for another bar. Charly's was a British-style pub with outdoor seating, and it seemed that most of the guys from the outbound Bikeshuttle journey had also been sent in this direction. They filled most of the outside seating area and were busy sharing tales of their journey.

We grabbed some drinks and those that hadn't eaten went in search of takeaway food that the bar staff had indicated could be eaten outside. The drinks were paid for and while earlier we had been subject to the local practice of closing the kitchen in the afternoon, I felt we now, in this pub environment, had an advantage over the locals. The bar ran a 'Service Anglais' and little signs adorned all the tables, advising our European friends of how service is done in England.

1. Go to the bar, order your drink and 'pay as you go'.
2. Take a seat wherever you wish or remain at the bar.
3. Repeat No. 1 as many times as you feel like it…

I did wonder if the locals thought this practice, something so familiar to us, to be a novelty. Without need for instruction, we did repeat No. 1 many, many times, before returning on foot to the hotel.

Brian at this stage was leaving us. Together with his wife, they ran a small mobile bar catering for weddings and other outdoor events. With a wedding booked for Saturday, he was taking a Friday-night flight back to the UK, and with his bike booked on to the lorry he would return to the depot on the Sunday to collect his K1300S.

We said our goodbyes to Brian, and it was the last supper (the kitchen of the Italian had re-opened) before we would all depart in the morning. With Brian already gone, Nick and

I would be taking a flight back to the UK. Dan and Shane would be heading back to Indiana, via Chicago, Schiphol and Reykjavik, hoping for less drama than their inbound journey; and Greg and Eddie would return to North Carolina via Heathrow, JFK and Charlotte. Not showing too much fatigue from the boozy afternoon and evening, we finally retired. We'd rinsed as much from the day as possible, but the closure of the bar forced our departure. Darkness had fallen, and we strolled back to the hotel in the warm evening air.

Chapter Eleven

Returning Home

Nick and I were on an early-morning flight from Geneva, which would give us ample time to be driven back to the depot from the airport and to ride the bikes back home. We had just enough time to grab a coffee before our shuttle bus collected us from the front of the hotel. We were joined by Dan, Shane, Greg and Eddie for the final farewell. Disposing of our very British handshakes, we exchanged manly hugs and slaps on the backs, and with that, we were in the bus and on the way to the airport. I hoped it would not be long before we once again met up. The distance over the Atlantic proves to be an unfortunate hinderance, but one that would never hinder our bond.

The flight took us out of Geneva with an opportunity to gaze out of the window and across the lake. From the lofty viewpoint, I could clearly see the Geneva Water Fountain 'Jet d'Eau', pumping half a cubic metre of water per second 140m into the air. The plane banked and the waters fell out of view as I settled back for the relatively short flight back to Luton.

Back in the UK, we made swift progress through the airport and exited to make our way to the meeting point where we would be picked up to collect the bikes. After the first bus filled and departed, there were a few moments of concern that we may have been forgotten, but a second standby transport soon arrived and we headed to the depot

I was glad to see the bike lined up on our arrival. It had only been twenty-four hours, but I was ready to get back in the saddle for one last ride to put a full stop at the end of such a successful and enjoyable Alps tour. We gathered our riding gear from the red boxes laid out alongside the lorry and were soon back on the road.

It felt strange to be back on the left-hand side of the UK roads. The landscape was flat and uninspiring in sharp contrast to the terrain we had been riding through just the day prior. Picking up the M1, then M6, we made our way north towards Manchester. We only stopped briefly for fuel before, just south of my final destination, Nick waved, peeled off and I was alone with my bike, the road home and my thoughts.

I arrived home safely, greeting my wife, who had been expecting my imminent return, and without unpacking, put the bike in the garage. That would be a job for another day. I took off my riding gear, tossing it over the bike. I stowed my boots and helmet, reached for some shorts. I grabbed a beer and climbed into the warm waters of our hot tub. It was time to start planning the next trip.

Afterword

Dan's journey home did indeed turn out to be eventful as his outward journey. Having arrived at the airport, he was informed that not only would he be on a different interconnecting flight to Shane, it would not be departing until a day later.

He returned alone to the hotel at Thoiry. Booked back into a room and spent his evening in the company of a pizza, while he updated every one of his misfortunes on Facebook.

He did finally get away the following day and, after many hours of travelling by air and finally by truck, finished his adventure.

Routes

Geneva to Grenoble	https://bit.ly/2kOrFbw
Grenoble to Martigny	https://bit.ly/2mkOjZP
Martigny to Curaglia	https://bit.ly/2kCxLvQ
Curaglia to Val Müstair	https://bit.ly/2koLUww
Val Müstair to Prata	
Camportacio	https://bit.ly/2lPUncv
Prata Camportacio to Bedretto	https://bit.ly/2lRK9Is
Bedretto to Grindelwald	https://bit.ly/2kCpwQs
Grindelwald to Geneva	https://bit.ly/2lQ84bo

Find more at https://www.redsmartie.com